IBEW Electrical Aptitude Practice Test: Training Manual and Study Guide with Practice

& Skills Test Published on Amazon

Introduction

The International Brotherhood of Electrical Workers designed the IBEW aptitude test is designed to assess candidates skills in algebra and reading comprehension.

To help you ace the test, we have created this book with 300 sample questions and explanations. You will get to practice your skills and learn the test format. However, these are not the exact questions you will face on the test, but they are similar and based on the same topics.

About the IBEW

The test consists of two sections.

1. Algebra and Functions
   a. 33 Questions in 46 minutes
2. Reading Comprehension
   a. 36 Questions in 51 minutes

What is a Good Score?

To qualify for most apprenticeships, you need to score at least 4 out of 9 on the test. Sometimes, the cut-off score can be higher if there are many applicants. So you should aim for a high score. This gives you a better chance of getting called by a recruiter, who usually start with the top scorers. Doing well is in your best interest.

Test Layout – Algebra & Functions

The Algebra & Functions sections covers the following topics:

- Whole Numbers
- Fractions
- Decimals
- Integers
- Rational and Irrational Numbers
- Exponents
- Equations, Formulas, and Inequalities
- Ratios, Rates, and Proportions
- The Cartesian Plane
- Systems of Equations
- Number series
- Factoring

Calculators are **NOT** allowed during the actual test; however, you will be provided scratch paper to work problems out on.

Test Layout – Reading Comprehension

This section consists of short passages followed by multiple-choice questions that measure your ability to interpret information from a written passage.

Test Tips

- Read the questions and answers carefully, eliminate as many options as possible.
- Do not leave answers blank. Blank answers and wrong answers are treated the same. There is no penalty to guess.
- Know your multiplication tables
- Don't try to cheat
- There are NO trick questions
- Keep practicing
- Practice without using a calculator. You will not be able to use a calculator for the actual test.
- Use the test to take the test. That means use the multiple-choice options you are given to help you answer questions quickly
- Be mindful of your time.

The Day Before

- Eat healthy and try to get a good night's sleep.
- Familiarize yourself with how to get to the testing location and associated travel time considering traffic or unexpected delays.

On Test Day

- Eat breakfast and do some brief physical activity to keep your brain fed and your mental agility up.
- Avoid drinking too much water or coffee so that you do not have to use the bathroom during the test.
- Arrival at the test site with plenty of time to spare
- Relax, you know the format of the test and the types of questions which will be asked.
- Have confidence in yourself!

Algebra & Functions

1. What is the product of (x+7)(x-4)?
   - A. $x^2-3x+28$
   - B. $x^2+11x-12$
   - C. $x^2+3x-28$
   - D. $x^2-12x+14$

2. What number comes next in the series: 12, 24, 48 , _?_
   - A. 72
   - B. 86
   - C. 96
   - D. 102

3. If A=5 and B=14 solve for C in:

$$A = \frac{B \times 15}{C}$$

   - A. 8
   - B. 24
   - C. 36
   - D. 42

4. Find the quotient of:

$$\frac{1.29}{6}$$

   - A. 0.0215
   - B. 0.215
   - C. 2.15
   - D. 21.5

5. Find 15% of 80
   - A. 12
   - B. 18
   - C. 22
   - D. 26

6. What is the value of x?

$$\frac{x}{6} = \frac{x}{2} - \frac{4}{3}$$

A. 2
B. 4
C. 6
D. 8

7. Which of the following statements is always true:

$$6A = B - 6$$

A. If A is less than −1, B is positive
B. If A is greater than −6, B is negative
C. If A is greater than −1, B is positive
D. If A is greater than −6, B is positive

8. How many 2.5ft segments can be made from a chord that is 35ft long?
A. 12
B. 13
C. 14
D. 15

9. Which system of equations is shown in the graph?

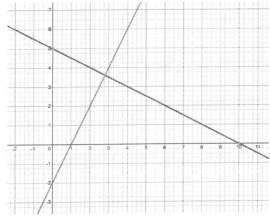

A. $y = 2x - 2$
$y = -0.5x + 5$

B. $y = -0.5x - 2$
$y = 2 + 5$

C. $y = -2x - 0.5$
$y = 5x + 2$

D. $y = -2x + 2$
$y = 5x - 0.5$

10. Solve for x:

$$\frac{x}{72 - x} = \frac{2}{7}$$

    A. 15
    B. 16
    C. 17
    D. 18

11. Mory earns $36.75 after working 3.5 hours. What is his hourly wage?
    A. $10.00
    B. $10.50
    C. $10.75
    D. $12.00

12. What is the quotient of:

$$\frac{10}{3} \div \frac{2}{3}$$

    A. 3
    B. 4
    C. 5
    D. 6

13. A floor measures 9 feet by 12 feet. How many square feet is the floor?
    A. 68 ft^2
    B. 89 ft^2
    C. 108 ft^2
    D. 118 ft^2

14. Simplify: $6xy-(3xy-3x^2)$
    A. $3xy+3x^2$
    B. $2x^2-3xy$
    C. $3x^2-3xy$
    D. $3xy+2x^2$

15. A deck of cards has 4 spades, 3 hearts, 7 clubs, and 10 diamonds. What is the probability that a spade will be picked?
    A. 1/5
    B. 1/6
    C. 1/8
    D. 1/9

16. Which option has the largest value?
    A. 8 dimes
    B. 3 quarters
    C. 79 pennies
    D. 15 nickels

17. Find the product of:

$$2.56$$
$$\times \ \underline{0.2}$$

    A. 0.342
    B. 0.512
    C. 3.42
    D. 5.12

18. What is 70% of 800
    A. 560
    B. 624
    C. 688
    D. 710

19. Kayla has a coupon for 12% off one frozen turkey. If each turkey costs $10, how much will Kayla pay if she buys two turkeys?
    A. $1.08
    B. $2.16
    C. $17.44
    D. $18.80

20. Solve and round to the nearest hundredth:

$$4.389+126.7-14.65 = ?$$

    A. 116.3
    B. 116.43
    C. 116.44
    D. 116.5

21. Which expression will have a value of 25 when x=-2
    A. x^2+3x-7
    B. x^2-2x+9
    C. $x^2+7x-14$
    D. x^2-6x+9

22. What is the value of x?

$$\frac{4}{x} + \frac{2}{6} = \frac{5}{x}$$

   A. 3
   B. 4
   C. 5
   D. 6

23. Jeremy is twelve years older than Tim. The sum of their ages 5 years ago was 28. How old is Tim now?
   A. 13
   B. 16
   C. 19
   D. 25

24. The cost of milk rose from $2.50 to $2.80. What was the percent increase?
   A. 8.3%
   B. 10.7%
   C. 12%
   D. 30%

25. What is the product of:

$$\frac{5}{6} \times \frac{8}{9}$$

   A. 12/21
   B. 15/23
   C. 18/25
   D. 20/27

26. John can run 10 miles in 60 minutes. If he runs for 4 hours, how far will he have run?
   A. 40 miles
   B. 50 miles
   C. 60 miles
   D. 80 miles

27. What is the value of x?

$$2(x + 7) - 3(2x - 4) = -18$$

    A.   3
    B.   8
    C.   11
    D.   15

28. Gas costs $5.12 a gallon. If Jessie buys 8.5 gallons how much will he pay?
    A. $40.60
    B. $42.50
    C. $43.52
    D. $44.60

29. 35% of what number is equal to 14.
    A.   4
    B.   40
    C.   49
    D.   400

30. Which value is the largest?
    A.   16/54
    B.   36/78
    C.   4/9
    D.   46/80

31. A pizza costs $7. If 6 pizzas are ordered and shared among 6 friends. How much does each person owe if the cost is shared equally?
    A. $7
    B. $8
    C. $9
    D. $11

32. What number comes next in the series: 3, 3, 6, 18, 72, _?_
    A.   360
    B.   288
    C.   192
    D.   144

33. 6 horses can pull 3,486 pounds. How much can 7 horses pull?
    A.   3587 pounds
    B.   3824 pounds
    C.   4067 pounds
    D.   4218 pounds

34. What is 45% of 240
    A.   89
    B.   108
    C.   164
    D.   192

35. Which equation represents the graph below

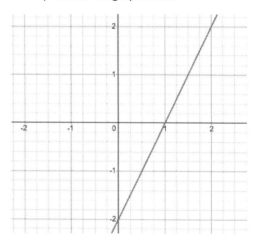

    A.   y=2x-2
    B.   y=4x+2
    C.   y=2x+2
    D.   y=4x-2

36. Find the product of:

$$388$$
$$\times\ 5.5$$

    A.   21.84
    B.   213.8
    C.   218.54
    D.   2134

37. If $x - y \neq 0$ then

$$\frac{x^2 - y^2}{x - y} =$$

A. x+y
B. x-y
C. x+2y
D. 2x-y

38. A tire makes 450 revolutions in a minute. How many times will the tire rotate in half an hour?

    A. 12,800
    B. 13,500
    C. 14,200
    D. 14,600

39. Calculate the sum of:

$$\frac{1}{2} + \frac{1}{6} + \frac{1}{12}$$

    A. 1/6
    B. 3/4
    C. 6/8
    D. 7/12

40. What number comes next in the series: 1, 4, 9, 16, 25, _?_

    A. 72
    B. 36
    C. 32
    D. 24

41. A poll states 80 out of 100 shoppers buy fresh fruit each week. If a store has 30,000 shoppers, how many can be expected to buy fresh fruit?

    A. 2,400
    B. 6,000
    C. 22,000
    D. 24,000

42. What is 41% of 1400

    A. 462
    B. 495
    C. 537
    D. 574

43. Sum:

$$2\sqrt{8} + 6\sqrt{2}$$

A. $10\sqrt{2}$
B. $6\sqrt{6}$
C. $6\sqrt{2}$
D. $6\sqrt{10}$

44. What value of x makes the equation true:

$$-12x - 2(x + 9) = 5(x + 4)$$

A. -4
B. -3
C. -2
D. -1

45. 18 is 15% of what number?
A. 75
B. 100
C. 120
D. 140

46. $140 is allocated for a party. If 80% of the money was spent, how much remains?
A. $24
B. $26
C. $28
D. $30

47. What is the value of x?

$$\frac{3}{4} - \frac{5x}{4} = \frac{108}{24}$$

A. -6
B. -3
C. 3
D. 6

48. Employees are paid $11.40 an hour. If an employee works over 40 hours, then they receive time and a half for every hour worked over the original 40. If an employee works 46 hours, how much will they be paid?
   A. $558.60
   B. $564.24
   C. $570.18
   D. $586.10

49. What number comes next in the series: 3, 2, 4, 3, 9, 8, 64, _?_
   A.   10
   B.   63
   C.   12
   D.   81

50. Factor:

$$6x^2 - 21x + 9$$

   A.   (2x+3)(3x+1)
   B.   (6x+7)(x+3)
   C.   (x-3)(6x-3)
   D.   (3x-7)(2x+3)

51. Simplify:

$$\frac{x^2 - x - 6}{x^2 - 2x - 8}$$

A. $\dfrac{x+3}{x+4}$ B. $\dfrac{-x-6}{-2x-8}$ C. $\dfrac{x+2}{x-4}$ D. $\dfrac{x-3}{x-4}$

52. Sarah is 28 years older than Vivian. In six years, Sarah will be three times as old as Vivian. What is Sarah's current age?
   A   30
   B.   32
   C.   34
   D.   36

53. What number comes next in the series: 5, 7, 15, 21, 45, _?_
    A. 54
    B. 63
    C. 75
    D. 86

54. What is 68% of 600
    A. 208
    B. 315
    C. 408
    D. 465

55. Solve for x:

$$\frac{5}{9}\left(2x - 7\right) = x$$

    A. 7
    B. 14
    C. 28
    D. 35

56. What statement is true about the following equation:

$$-9(x + 3) + 12 = -3(2x + 5) - 3x$$

    A. The equation has infinitely many solutions
    B. The equation has no solution
    C. The equation has one solution at x=0
    D. The equation has one solution at x=1

57. Factor the polynomial:

$$2x^2 - 6x - 56$$

    A. 2(x2-3x+18)
    B. 2(x+4) (x-7)
    C. 2(x-4) (x+7)
    D. (2x+7) (x-8)

58. Simplify:

$$26 - 7(3 + 5) \div 4 + 2$$

    A. 14
    B. 18
    C. 23
    D. 40

59. A greeting card company has a monthly overhead of $6,000. It costs 18 cents to print each card, and the cards sell for 30 cents each. How many cards must be sold each month for the company to make a profit?
    A. 30,000
    B. 40,000
    C. 50,000
    D. 60,000

60. A $220 coat is on sale for 30% off, what will the customer pay?
    A. $190
    B. $154
    C. $165
    D. $66

61. Find the sum of:

$$\frac{3}{9} + \frac{4}{6}$$

    A. 1/3
    B. 2/3
    C. 5/6
    D. 1

62. Simplify:

$$2 - 8 \div (2^4 \div 2)$$

    A. 1
    B. 2
    C. 3
    D. 6

63. The ratio of in state to out-of-state students is 15 to 2. If there are 750 in-state students, how many out-of-state students are there?
  A. 100
  B. 112
  C. 130
  D. 260

64. What number comes next in the series: 178, 156, 78, 56, 28, _?_
  A. -6
  B. 6
  C. 16
  D. 26

65. Find the quotient of:

$$\frac{1823.7}{5}$$

  A. 323.473
  B. 364.74
  C. 384.238
  D. 421.51

66. What is the value of x?

$$\frac{x}{2} + \frac{x}{6} = 4$$

  A. 1
  B. 2
  C. 3
  D. 6

67. 14 workers can complete a job in 156 hours. How long will it take 13 workers to complete the same job?
  A. 132 hours
  B. 144 hours
  C. 160 hours
  D. 168 hours

68. Which equation represents the graph below:

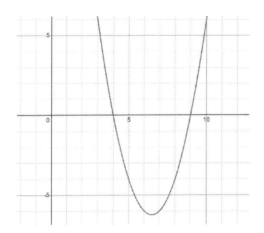

A. x²+13x+36

B. x²-13x+36

C. x²+6x-36

D. x²-6x+36

69. Solve: $x^5 x^2 + x^0$,when x=3

    A.   2142
    B.   2143
    C.   2187
    D.   2188

70. A rectangle is cut to create two squares that each have an area of 25. What is the perimeter of the original rectangle?

    A.   20
    B.   25
    C.   30
    D.   35

71. Simplify:

$$17^2$$

    A.   269
    B.   279
    C.   289
    D.   299

72. Simplify:

$$\sqrt{3}(5\sqrt{3} - \sqrt{12} + \sqrt{10})$$

A. $9 + \sqrt{30}$
B. $15 - \sqrt{15} + \sqrt{13}$
C. $15\sqrt{3} - 3\sqrt{12} + 3\sqrt{10}$
D. $3 - \sqrt{13}$

73. Mike types 3x as fast as Chris. Together they can type 24 pages an hour. If Chris could type as fast as Mike, how much more pages could they type in an hour?

A. 30 pages
B. 36 pages
C. 40 pages
D. 48 pages

74. Which option is a solution to:

$$x^2 + 12x + 36$$

A. $x = -6$
B. $x = -6, 6$
C. $x = 6$
D. $x = 0, 6$

75. A population of yeast grows from 10 to 320 in 5-hours. How fast does the yeast grow?

A. It doubles every hour
B. It triples every hour
C. It doubles every two hours
D. It triples every two hours

76. Simplify

$$4\frac{1}{5} + 2\frac{1}{5} + 3\frac{3}{10}$$

A. $9\frac{9}{10}$
B. $9\frac{7}{10}$
C. $9\frac{4}{5}$
D. $9\frac{6}{15}$

77. What comes next in the series: 4, 31, 8, 29, 16, 27, _?_

A. 32

B. 22
C. 46
D. 26

78. 18% of 250 is:
   A. 26
   B. 32
   C. 45
   D. 54

79. Inspectors sampled 50 parts from a lot of 400. Four articles from the sample were defective. What percentage of parts is faulty?
   A. 4%
   B. 8%
   C. 10%
   D. 12%

80. Simplify:

$$(a - b)(a^2 + ab + b^2) + a^3 + b^3$$

   A. 2a³
   B. 2a³+2b³
   C. 2a³-2ab
   D. 2a³+a2b

81. Factor the polynomial:

$$21x^2 - x - 2$$

   A. (x-7)(x+3)
   B. (2x+3)(x-7)
   C. (x+7)(7x+3)
   D. (7x+2)(3x-1)

82. Solve for x:

$$\frac{x - 5}{3} = \frac{x - 3}{5}$$

   A. 6
   B. 7
   C. 8
   D. 9

83. Which of the following is equivalent to:

$$\frac{35}{56}$$

A. 1/16
B. 5/8
C. 7/9
D. 12/15

84. Find the product of:

$$\frac{3}{8} \times \frac{4}{6}$$

A. 1/3
B. 1/4
C. 1/5
D. 1/6

85. Seven cars each need four new times. The cost to replace one tire is $68. How much will it cost (to the nearest dollar) to replace all tires if sales tax is 8%?

A. $1904
B. $2056
C. $2142
D. $2204

86. Which equation is equivalent to: 3(4x+6)(x-9)

A. 12x²-90x-162
B. 2x²+96x-62
C. 9x²-30x+54
D. 3x²+36x-108

87. Solve for x:

$$\frac{3}{4}(x+3) = 9$$

A. 3
B. 6
C. 7
D. 9

88. Subtract:

$$8\sqrt{28} - 3\sqrt{7}$$

    A. $7\sqrt{13}$
    B. $13\sqrt{7}$
    C. $16\sqrt{7}$
    D. $7\sqrt{16}$

89. What number is missing from the series: 7, 12, 19, 28, 39, _?_
    A. 42
    B. 47
    C. 52
    D. 56

90. Find the product of:

$$\begin{array}{r} 0.240 \\ \times\ \ 9.9 \\ \hline \end{array}$$

    A. 2.376
    B. 18.72
    C. 23.26
    D. 265.3

91. Solve

$$(-3)^3$$

    A. -9
    B. 9
    C. -27
    D. 27

92. A 15ft pole casts a 5ft shadow. How long will the shadow be for a 6ft pole?
    A. 0.5 ft
    B. 1 ft
    C. 1.5 ft
    D. 2 ft

93. If $6w + 4 = 8w$ then $4w = ?$

    A. 1
    B. 2
    C. 4
    D. 8

94. Which ordered pair is a solution to:

$$3a + b = 10$$
$$-4a - 2b = 2$$

    A. (23, -11)
    B. (11, -23)
    C. (14, -8)
    D. (8, -14)

95. 1 in 9 people voted for Party Alpha in an election. Everyone else voted for Party Bravo. In a town of 810 people, how many people voted for Bravo?

    A. 90
    B. 680
    C. 720
    D. 801

96. Simplify:

$$(2x + 5)(3x^2 - 2x - 4)$$

    A. 6x³+15x²+6x+12
    B. 21x²+22x-20
    C. 6x³+19x²+18x+20
    D. 6x³+11x²-18x-20

97. Solve for x

$$2x^2 - 8x - 24 = 0$$

    A. 8, -2
    B. 6, -4
    C. 6, 2
    D. 6, -2

98. A waiter earns 18% on tips. If they served $1,200 worth of food in a shift, how much in tips will they have made?

    A. $212

B. $216
C. $220
D. $224

99. A line passes through the points (-3,18) and (5,2). What is the slope of the line?
   A. -2
   B. -0.5
   C. 0.5
   D. 2

100. Which line is perpendicular to:

$$y = -5x + 27$$

A. $y = 5x - 27$
B. $y = -x/5 + 27$
C. $y = x/5 + 27$
D. $y = -x/5 - 27$

101. Rick is half as old as Steve, who is three times as old as Tom. The sum of their ages is 55. How old is Tom?
   A. 5
   B. 10
   C. 15
   D. 20

102. What number is missing from the series: 1, 2, 5, 10, 17, _?_
   A. 21
   B. 26
   C. 29
   D. 31

103. Simplify

$$\left(2x^4\right)\left(3x^6\right)$$

   A. 12x^{24}
   B. 24x^{12}
   C. 6x^{10}
   D. 6x^{24}

104. Tires cost $62 each. If four new tires are purchased at a 10% discount, how much will they save?
   A. $24.80
   B. $55.80
   C. $223.20
   D. $248.18

105. Factor the polynomial:

$$6x^2 - 6$$

   A. 6(x+1)(x-1)
   B. 6(x-1)(x+6)
   C. (2x+2)(3x+3)
   D. (2x-2)(3x+3)

106. Solve for x:

$$3(2x+6)+2x=10$$

   A. -2
   B. -1
   C. 1
   D. 2

107. 60 students register for a class. One fifth of the class are boys. How many girls are in the class?
   A. 12
   B. 24
   C. 26
   D. 48

108. Solve:

$$12(84 - 5) - (3 \times 54)$$

   A. 985
   B. 841
   C. 796
   D. 786

109. What is the value of y?

$$2x - 3y = 0$$
$$-4x + 2y = -8$$

A. 0
B. 2
C. 4
D. 6

110. A player scores in 8 of 20 attempts. What percentage is this?
  A. 8%
  B. 16%
  C. 32%
  D. 40%

111. Simplify:

$$2.5 \times 3^3$$

A. 22.5
B. 75
C. 67.5
D. 675

112. $y = 3ab + 2b^3$ what is y when a=1 and b=2?
  A. 16
  B. 18
  C. 20
  D. 22

113. Which is equivalent to:

$$3x^3y^5 + 3x^5y^3 - (4x^5y^3 - 3x^3y^5)$$

A. -x⁵y³
B. 6x⁵y³-x³y⁵
C. 7x⁵y³
D. 6x³y⁵-x⁵y³

114. 45% is equivalent to what fraction?
    A. 4/5
    B. 5/8
    C. 25/50
    D. 9/20

115. Was is the equation of a line that passes through (4, 1) and is parallel to y=4x-7
    A. y=2x-7
    B. y=4x-15
    C. y=4x+15
    D. y=2x+7

116. Which of the following is true:
    A. Parallel lines intersect at right angles
    B. Parallel lines never intersect
    C. Perpendicular lines never intersect
    D. Intersecting lines have 2 points in common

117. Find the quotient of:

$$\frac{338.56}{23}$$

    A. 1.469
    B. 12.49
    C. 14.72
    D. 26.82

118. What is a 12% tax on a $15 purchase?
    A. $0.86
    B. $1.25
    C. $1.42
    D. $1.80

119. 44 is 80% of what number?
    A. 51
    B. 53
    C. 55
    D. 57

120. A swimming pool is 9ft deep, 25ft long, and 15ft wide. What is the volume of the pool?

A. 1500 ft²
B. 3375 ft²
C. 3825 ft²
D. 4250 ft²

121. What is the midpoint of (-20, 8) and (4, 4)?
 A. (-8, 6)
 B. (-8, 12)
 C. (8, -6)
 D. (8, -12)

122. A 24ft pole casts an 8ft shadow. A nearby pole is 72ft. How long is its shadow?
 A. 16fg
 B. 24ft
 C. 32ft
 D. 56ft

123. A motorcycle costs $7,250. If it depreciates at a rate of 12% a year, how much will it be worth after one year?
 A. $870
 B. $1,250
 C. $5,920
 D. $6,380

124. What number is missing from the series: 2, 9, 3, 8, 4, 7, _?_
 A. 5
 B. 6
 C. 10
 D. 12

125. Consider the formula:

$$y = 3(x + 5)(x - 2)$$

Which of option is equivalent to the equation above

 A. y=x²-9x+10
 B. y=3x²+9x-30
 C. y=6x²+18+30
 D. y=3x²-6x-6

126. Find the quotient of:

$$5 \div \frac{30}{36}$$

    A. 3
    B. 4
    C. 5
    D. 6

127. If Lydia's height is $\frac{2}{a}$ of Francine's height and Francine is b inches tall, how tall is Lydia?

    A. $\frac{2}{ab}$
    B. $2(ab)$
    C. $2\frac{a}{b}$
    D. $\frac{2b}{a}$

128. What is 30% of 40?
    A. 8
    B. 12
    C. 14
    D. 15

129. Solve for x:

$$5^{11} = 5^2 \times 5^x$$

    A. 3
    B. 6
    C. 9
    D. 12

130. Which number is greatest?

$$0.6, \frac{2}{3}, \frac{13}{22}, 0.08$$

    A. 0.6
    B. 2/3
    C. 13/22
    D. 0.08

131. What is the value of x and y?

$$2x + 7y = 4$$
$$3x + 5y = -5$$

A. (-5, 2)
B. (-2, 5)
C. (2, 5)
D. (5, -2)

132. Simplify

$$(7y^2 + 3xy - 9) - (2y^2 + 3xy - 5)$$

A. 5y²+4
B. 9y²+6xy-14
C. 5y²+6xy-14
D. 5y²-4

133. Which is equivalent to:

$$6.6 \times 10^{-4}$$

A. 0.000066
B. 0.00066
C. 0.0066
D. 0.066

134. Solve for x:

$$\frac{x}{-4} + 3 = -7$$

A. 4
B. 12
C. 28
D. 40

135. What is the equation of a line that passes through (0,-1) and (2,3)
A. y=2x+1
B. y=2x-1
C. y=x-1
D. y=x+1

136. Convert 24% to a fraction
    A. 6/25
    B. 4/25
    C. 6/24
    D. 4/24

137. One gallon of paint covers 400ft². How many gallons are required to cover a 6,400 ft² office?
    A. 8 gallons
    B. 12 gallons
    C. 16 gallons
    D. 18 gallons

138. What number is missing from the series: 2, 5, 9, 19, _?_
    A. 22
    B. 28
    C. 34
    D. 37

139. Tim is paid $26 after working 8 hours. How much will he get paid after working 37 hours?
    A. $118.5
    B. $120.25
    C. $127
    D. $135

140. Find the product of:

$$520 \times 0.97$$

    A. 45.78
    B. 50.44
    C. 457.8
    D. 504.4

141. What is 22% of 150
    A. 22
    B. 28
    C. 33
    D. 38

142. If 1 inch of chain costs $0.14, then 3.5ft will cost?
    A. $4.25
    B. $5.88
    C. $6.32
    D. $6.96

143. A bag contains 105 jellybeans: 23 white, 23 red, 14 purple, 26 yellow, and 19 green. What is the probability of selecting either a yellow or a green jellybean?
    A. 3/7
    B. 1/6
    C. 1/12
    D. 2/9

144. Simplify:

$$\sqrt{6^2 + 8^2}$$

    A. 7
    B. 10
    C. 14
    D. 100

145. What is 42.5% of 200?
    A. 65
    B. 75
    C. 85
    D. 95

146. Simplify:

$$(3x^4 + 3x^2 - x + 5) - 3(x^4 + x^3 - 2x^2 - 6)$$

    A. $6x^4+3x^3+5x^2-x-13$
    B. $3x^3+3x^2-x-13$
    C. $3x^4-3x^3+9x^2-x+23$
    D. $-3x^3+9x^2-x+23$

147. What was the average speed, if it took 9 hours to travel 540 miles.
    A. 90 miles per hour
    B. 80 miles per hour
    C. 60 miles per hour
    D. 100 miles per hour

148. How many solutions exist for the following system of equations:

$$4a + b = 5$$
$$8a + 2b = -6$$

A.   Infinitely many solutions
B.   No solutions
C.   1 solution
D.   2 solutions

149. What is the value of x?

$$\frac{1}{3x} + \frac{5}{12} = \frac{2}{x}$$

A.   4
B.   5
C.   6
D.   8

150. What number is missing from the series: 2, 5, 14, 41, _?_
A.   18
B.   54
C.   122
D.   168

Reading Comprehension
Read each passage carefully and answer the question that follow.

Hearsay, is secondhand reporting. It is only admissible in court when the truth regarding a statement is irrelevant. For example, a defendant might claimed to have been unconscious. But, a witness testifies that the defendant spoke to them during that period. Here, the truth of what the defendant said is irrelevant; thus, the evidence is admissible. This is because the witness appears in court and swears an oath to tell the truth.

151. What is the purpose of the passage?
A.   Explain why hearsay is unfair to the accused
B.   Question the truthfulness of hearsay
C.   Argue that the rules of hearsay should be changed
D.   Specify when hearsay is admissible and why

152. How is the acceptable use of hearsay explained?
    A. By listing a set of criteria
    B. Providing a hypothetical example
    C. Citing the Constitution
    D. Citing case law

153. When is hearsay admissible in court?
    A. When the statement is a fact
    B. When the statement is true
    C. When the truth of the statement doesn't matter
    D. When the statement is false

Before a home or business makes exterior modifications, owners are required to receive approval from the Design Control Board. Renovations, new developments, landscaping, signage, and painting are all subject to review. The board has the authority to approve, modify, or deny all exterior modification proposals. Some projects may require additional permits depending on the type work.

154. Which of the following statements is true:
    A. Landscape remodeling is subject to review
    B. Once the board approves a request, no other permits are required
    C. Interior remodeling is subject to review by the board
    D. Businesses are not subject to the review

All bus drivers with more than two years of experience need to complete twenty hours of training in the next ten months. The training will focus on how to handle the vehicle in different situations. The training will use a simulator, which is a better way to learn and practice driving skills to develop safe driving habits. Drivers are also be able to test their reflexes and coordination under various scenarios without risking personal injury or property damage.

155. Bus drivers are required to do which of the following?
    A. Learn how to drive defensively and operate the new computer
    B. Complete 10 months of refresher training
    C. Train new drivers on using the simulator
    D. Complete 20 hours of training on a simulator

156. What is the purpose of the refresher training?
    A. Ensure all bus drivers maintain proper habits
    B. Give experienced drivers the opportunity to learn new skills
    C. Help all drivers maintain hand eye coordination
    D. Save money

Clarkson City recently distributed recycling containers to all households. Each container was accompanied by a letter that read: "We prefer that you use this container as your new primary recycling bin. Additional recycling containers may be purchased from the city."

157. Each household should:
    A. Only use one container
    B. Must use the new recycling container
    C. Use the new recycling container
    D. Has to buy the new recycling container

158. Which of the following is true regarding the containers?
    A. The new containers are better
    B. Only the new containers can be used
    C. The new containers hold more
    D. People can use other containers

Rock salt is a common substance that is used to treat the streets after snow or ice falls. It helps to melt the ice and make the roads safer. Sometimes, rock salt is mixed with calcium chloride. This mixture works better than rock salt alone when the temperature is very low and the ice is thick. It is also better for the environment, because it uses less salt and reduces the damage to plants and animals.

159. Which of the following is not a consideration when deciding to use rock salt or salt and calcium chloride?
    A. Temperature
    B. Environment
    C. Ice
    D. Amount of traffic on the road

160. According to the passage, which of the following is true?
    A. Salt and calcium chloride is most effective when the temperature is below 0
    B. It must stop snowing before the roads are treated
    C. Major roads are salted first
    D. Sand is applied when there is a light amount of snow

City ordinance requires dogs that are four months or older to be tested and treated for rabies every 6 months. Owners will receive a certificate once the test is complete and are encouraged to attach it to the dog's collar to show that the dog has been vaccinated. This also helps Animal control to reunite owners with their dogs should you become separated.

161. What does the passage imply?
     A.   Dogs that do not have the certificate attached are more likely to be lost
     B.   A dog that has a certificate attached to its collar is more likely to be reunited with its owner
     C.   Dogs that have not been vaccinated will not be returned to their owners
     D.   Owners are required to attach the rabies certificate to the dog's collar

Journalists often have to report on tragic events, such as terrorism, poverty, natural disasters, and death. These events can cause a lot of stress, which can have adverse health effects. Managers should look out for signs of stress in their staff. Research shows that events caused by humans (such as violent crime, war, car crashes, etc.) are harder to cope with than events caused by nature. The more journalists see these events, the more likely they are to have problems with stress in the future.

162. What is the main idea of the passage?
     A.   Managers must be aware and look for signs of stress in their staff
     B.   Witnessing a tragic event will result in a stress disorder
     C.   The more one witnesses tragic events, the more likely they are to have a stress disorder
     D.   Journalists have an elevated risk of exposure to dramatic events

163. Which of the following scenarios should managers pay particular attention to
     A.   Witnessing extreme poverty
     B.   Returning from overseas travel
     C.   Supporting a natural disaster relief fund
     D.   Exposure to a tragedy caused by humans

164. What is an action a manager could take to reduce the risk for journalists?
     A.   Rotate journalists to reduce the frequency and number of tragic event exposures
     B.   Give journalists extra time off
     C.   Have therapists travel with journalists
     D.   Give journalists hazard pay

Community policing is a popular idea for reforming urban law enforcement in the last ten years. It was first proposed by Commissioner Lee Brown of Houston in 1983, who thought that police officers should be accessible to the communities they serve. This accessibility is created by having police officers patrol on foot rather than in cars. By constantly assigning police officers to the same area, the hope is that officers can build rapport with the residents to create and foster a network of trust. In theory, this trust helps empower residents and other community members to support police intervention in reducing criminal activity. Cities that have implanted this style of policing have had mixed results. While some communities have successfully implemented it others have experienced resistance from both citizens and officers.

165. Community policing has been in use since:
    A. 1970s
    B. 1980s
    C. The Carter administration
    D. Since Lee Brown was New York City Police commissioner

166. The phrase network of trust suggests:
    A. Police can rely on one another
    B. The community can rely on the police to protect them
    C. The police and community can rely on one another
    D. The community can rely on itself for support

167. The best title for this article would be:
    A. Community Policing: The Solution to Crime
    B. Houston sets the Pace in Community Policing
    C. Partners for Peace: Communities and Cops
    D. Community Policing: An uncertain Future?

Burns come in three types: first, second, and third degree. Firefighters need to know each type so they can apply correct medical care. First-degree burns are not serious and causes the skin redden, but not blister. A mild sunburn is an example. These burns usually do not need medical care beyond being cooled.

Second-degree burns cause blisters on the skin and should be immediately treated. The burned area should be soaked in warm water and then covered with a clean bandage. (Do not apply butter or grease, as this increases the chances of infection). If the burn covers a large part of the body, the victim should be taken to the hospital right away.

Third-degree burns are the most serious. The skin may turn black or white and look charred. These burns often occur after contact with flames and can quickly become infected. These burns should not be put in water nor should burned clothing be removed. If possible, put clean dressings on the burn and take the victim to the hospital.

168. The best title for this article would be
    A. Treating third degree burns
    B. Recognizing and treating different types of burns
    C. Categories of burns
    D. Preventing infections in burns

169. How should second-degree burns be treated?
    A. With butter or grease
    B. Nothing
    C. With warm water
    D. With cold water

170. What color do first-degree burns turn the skin?
    A. Red
    B. Blue

C. Black
D. White

171. What is the main idea of the passage?
    A. There are different types of burns
    B. Firefighters should always carry cold compresses
    C. Different types of burns need to be treated differently
    D. Butter or grease can help heal burns

Irritable patients can be a challenge for even the most talented healthcare worker. It is important to remain calm and not take insults personally. Patients are often not actually mad at you, but are rather venting their frustration at something else on you. If you react in an irritable way to these patients, you will make them more hostile and make treatment harder. Some patients might try to intentionally get under your skin to provoke a reaction.

172. According to the passage, which statement is true?
    A. Irritable patients are common in the health care industry
    B. Irritable patients only challenge new healthcare workers
    C. Irritable patients are personally angry at you
    D. Responding to irritable patients in a like manner will make treatment challenging

173. What does the passage suggest about healthcare workers?
    A. They easily lose control of their emotions
    B. Should not talk with patients
    C. May provide inadequate treatment if they themselves become angry
    D. They must be careful as the patient is likely to sue the hospital

174. What best describes the writer's view regarding irate patients?
    A. Irate patients want your attention
    B. Irate patients are miserable
    C. Irate patients should be forced to wait for treatment
    D. An irate patient can ruin your career

The broken window theory is a way of explaining how small acts of vandalism can lead to bigger acts of crime. But it can also be used to understand other situations in society. The theory says that if a window in an empty building Is broken and no one fixes it, then soon all the windows will be broken. Once all windows are broken, the building has a higher chance of being robbed or being set on fire.

The same thing can happen in the workplace. If an employee does something wrong and no one corrects them, then other employees will start doing the same thing or worse and cause a management crisis. For example, if an employee is rude to a manager, others might also be rude to the manager. People will think, "if they can get away with it, why can't I?" What starts as a small problem can become a big problem overnight.

175. Which of the following could happen overnight?
    A. The building will burn down
    B. All the windows will be broken
    C. A management crisis could occur
    D. Another building will have broken windows

176. What is the main idea of the passage?
    A. Minor infractions should result in disciplinary action
    B. Broken windows should immediately be repaired
    C. People shouldn't be disrespectful
    D. Derelict property should carefully be watched

177. The passage suggests:
    A. The broken window theory is incomplete
    B. Managers need to learn how to handle crisis
    C. People are lazy
    D. People will get away with what they can

Over the past several weeks, supervisors have received complaints about buses running hot. Every bus route has checkpoints for drivers to evaluate their timing. Drivers are reminded that if they are ahead of schedule, they should wait at a checkpoint until the appropriate departure time.

178. According to the passage, what does a bus running hot mean?
    A. The engine is overheating
    B. The bus is ahead of schedule
    C. The inside of the bus is warm
    D. There is no room for passengers

179. According to the passage:
    A. Every stop is a checkpoint
    B. Customer complaints should be minimized
    C. Drivers usually arrive and depart early from their stops
    D. Each route has points they can use to check their timing

Drivers have to refuel their trucks at the end of each shift. The maintenance department will take care of everything else and keep track of the service records. If a truck needs to be fixed, drivers should fill out a pink repair form and give it to the shift supervisor.

180. Who will perform an oil change on the truck?
    A. The maintenance department
    B. Drivers
    C. Supervisors

D.   Contractors

181. The passage suggests:
    A.   Trucks are refueled when less than half full
    B.   Oil is to be changed every 1,000 miles
    C.   Trucks are refueled at the end of each shift
    D.   Frequently need to be repaired

Hazardous waste is defined as any waste designated by the U.S. Environmental Protection Agency (EPA) as hazardous. If an employee is unsure if a package is hazardous, they should immediately stop what they are doing and notify the closest supervisor for guidance.

182. What is hazardous waste?
    A.   Anything dangerous for workers to handle
    B.   Anything requiring special trucks
    C.   Anything designated by the EPA
    D.   Anything not allowed in the city garbage

183. A worker comes sees a container of unlabeled cleaning solvents, they should:
    A.   Assume the material is safe
    B.   Leave a note asking for the container to be labeled
    C.   Contact a supervisor
    D.   Leave the container and move on

People often hesitate when adopting a retired racing greyhound because they mistakenly believe these animals require a lot of space or have a lot of health issues. These fears are far from true as greyhounds have a mild disposition and prefer to sprint rather than run great distances. They can get enough exercise with just a few laps around an average sized backyard. Greyhounds are great with children and other dogs (as well as cats). They are extremely loving and loyal creatures. However, because of these behaviors, they are not great watchdogs.

184. What type of people should adopt a greyhound?
    A.   People who don't have children
    B.   Those who live in an apartment
    C.   People who don't like dogs
    D.   People who own a dog or cat

185. What is a drawback to adopting a greyhound?
    A.   They are not watchdogs
    B.   They are old
    C.   They are extremely competitive
    D.   They require a lot of space in order to run

A simple way to plan healthy menus is to shop on the outer aisles of grocery stores where fresh fruit, vegetables, dairy, and meat products can be found. In most stores, processed foods, such as chips, cookies, snacks, candy, and soda are located in the inner aisles. Grains, such as pasta, bread, rice, and cereal are often located on the outside aisles next to the fruits and meats. This method of shopping is also often faster than walking down every aisle.

186. What is the best title for this article?
    A. Why people should shop in health stores
    B. How to quickly shop
    C. How to shop for healthy food
    D. How to cook healthy food

187. What is the best way to shop?
    A. By making a list
    B. Shop along the outer aisles
    C. Price hunting
    D. Clipping coupons

188. Why is the temptation to buy unhealthy items reduced?
    A. The items aren't on sale
    B. They are harder to find
    C. Health stores don't generally have junk food
    D. You aren't walking past aisles containing these items

To become a veterinarian, a candidate must pass both a national and state exam. The state exam is specific to each state. Many people feel the state exam is unnecessary. They argue that passing the national medical board should be sufficient. Others, however, believe state boards are necessary so veterinarians know how to treat local issues/conditions specific to the area they practice in.

189. A veterinarian must?
    A. Pass only the national medical board
    B. Graduate from an accredited program
    C. Be knowledgeable about medical issues in all states
    D. Pass both the national and state exam

190. What is the best tile for the passage?
    A. State Exams Deemed Irrelevant
    B. Pet Owners Guide to Veterinarians
    C. Pros and Cons of Veterinarian Requirements
    D. How to Become a veterinarian

191. State exams are important because:
    A. The presence of regional diseases
    B. They provide extra practice
    C. They maintain standards for the medical community
    D. They hold veterinarians to a higher standard

The northern hemisphere tilts towards the sun during the summer months. This makes the days longer and the temperatures warmer than in winter. In the northern hemisphere, the summer solstice marks the first day of summer and is the longest day of the year. However, the same day, June 21, is the beginning of winter in the southern hemisphere, which is now facing away from the sun and is called the winter solstice.

192. When its summer in the northern hemisphere, the southern hemisphere is experiencing:
    A. Spring
    B. Summer
    C. Fall
    D. Winter

193. We can infer the summer solstice occurs on what date?
    A. 21 July
    B. 21 June
    C. 21 November
    D. 21 December

When police officers arrest someone, they have to read them their Miranda Rights. This is to make sure that the person knows their legal rights and does not say anything that can be used against them in court. If the police officers question the person without reading them their rights, the court may throw out the case.

194. What is the main idea of the passage?
    A. Officers must be careful when questioning individuals
    B. People can mistakenly believe they are in custody when they are not
    C. Officers questioning a suspect should not give the suspect the impression they are being taken into custody
    D. Miranda Rights do not need to be read to all suspects

195. When must Miranda Rights be read to a suspect?
    A. During questioning
    B. When placing someone under arrest
    C. Before taking someone to the police station
    D. Before releasing a suspect

Bob's Burger is a new lunch spot in Old Town Center, where it moved from the North Quarter. It has three lunch specials every day, with different combos to choose from at affordable prices. You can order from a cashier at a stand-up counter and then pick up your food. You can sit at one of the four tables that are shared with other customers and enjoy your meal.

196. If you eat at Bob's Burger, you can expect:
   A. Surrounded by antiques
   B. A waiter to take your order
   C. To have to carry your food to a table
   D. To be asked on a date

197. What is the purpose of the passage?
   A. Talk about the owner of Bob's Burger
   B. Describe the type of food served
   C. Encourage people to eat at Bob's Burger
   D. Explain the historical significance of the city

There are two types of diabetes, insulin-dependent and non-insulin dependent. Most of the 13-14M people in the US who have diabetes are non-insulin dependent. This is known as Type II diabetes. Symptoms develop gradually, which makes it hard to initially identify. This is why approximately half the people who have diabetes are not aware they have it. This is very dangerous as diabetes can cause damage to the heart, eyes, kidneys, blood vessels, and nervous system if not treated. Both Type I and Type II diabetes have different causes and short-term treatments, but they have the same adverse long-term health effects.

198. What is the most dangerous aspect of Type II diabetes?
   A. Daily insulin shots are required
   B. The pancreas does not produce enough insulin
   C. Diabetes interferes with digestion
   D. People may not know they have it

199. What is the same for both Type I and II diabetes?
   A. Long term treatment
   B. Long term health effects
   C. Short term health treatment
   D. Causes

Adolescent crimes are likely to be committed by offenders who are the same age, sex, and race as that of the victim. Preventing adolescent violence is a twofold problem that can be resolved through new violence protection programs in urban middle schools. The program teaches both victims and agitators conflict resolution skills and how to solve conflict without violence. This helps change the idea that violence and revenge cause increased respect in ones peer group.

200. What is the main idea of the passage?
   A. Violence prevention programs in middle schools are designed to reduce the adolescent crime rate
   B. Adolescents are more likely to commit crimes than adults
   C. Middle school students should attend crime prevention programs
   D. Violence among adolescents is increasing

201. Why is preventing violence a twofold problem?
    A. Adolescents are equally likely to be victims of crime as other age groups
    B. Adolescents must be stopped from being both the victim and the aggressor
    C. Adolescents must change both their behavior and their perception of violence
    D. Adolescents are vulnerable and reluctant to change

Scientific Services LLC is the largest crime lab in the US, with more than 250 employees. The lab was accredited by the Laboratory Accreditation board in 1980 and started processing samples in 1981. Since then, it has handled over 150,000 specimens. The local Sheriff's Department sends half of the samples to the lab, and the rest come from state and federal agencies. The company offers forensic services to all the police organizations in San Diego County.

202. According to the passage, which statement is true?
    A. The lab is the largest of its kind in the country
    B. The lab started processing samples in 1981
    C. The lab started processing samples in 1980
    D. The number of samples the lab processes has increased over the years

The camera has a mechanism called the shutter that controls how much light gets to the film. It works like a valve that opens and closes for a short time. The shutter speed is how long the shutter stays open, measured in fractions of a second. When you take a picture, you should keep the camera as steady as possible. If the shutter is open for too long, the picture can get blurry. With SLR cameras, you can usually hold the camera without blurring the picture if the shutter speed is 1/30 of a second or faster.

203. What is true about camera shutters?
    A. They freeze motion
    B. They prevent blurry photos
    C. They serve as light valves
    D. They make handheld shots difficult

204. The shutter works in conjunction with
    A. Time
    B. Space
    C. Dials
    D. Demand

205. Which of the following is likely to result in blurry photos?
    A. An SLR camera
    B. When a large amount of light is exposed
    C. A shutter speed of 1/60
    D. A slow shutter speed

Retribution and deterrence are two theories on how to punish criminals. Retribution means that the punishment should fit the crime and be fair. Deterrence means that the punishment should stop future crimes by making potential criminals afraid of the consequences. According to deterrence, the punishment does not have to match the crime, but should be universally applied. This way, other criminals will know what will happen to them if they commit the same crime.

206. The passages suggests that if a person who believes the death penalty results in fewer murders most likely also believes:
    A. Deterrence theory
    B. Retribution
    C. Integrity of the justice system
    D. Compassion

207. A person who believes in deterrence theory most likely supports:
    A. Unanimous jury verdicts
    B. Early release of prisoners
    C. A broad definition of the insanity defense
    D. Allowing television cameras into the court room

City law says that garbage containers should not weigh more than fifty pounds. Workers should decide for themselves if a container is too heavy. If they think it is, drivers should leave a printed warning on the container. The warning tells the owner that the container is too heavy, and that they need to make it lighter for the garbage to be picked up.

208. How will workers determine if a container is overweight?
    A. Using a scale
    B. Practicing lifting 50 pounds so they know what it feels like
    C. Assume anything they can lift is less than 50 pounds
    D. Using his or her best guess

209. What are the repercussions of having a container weighing more than 50 pounds?
    A. A warning will be attached to the container and the garbage will not be collected
    B. The household will be fined
    C. A special truck will need to be called to pick up the container
    D. The garbage will be collected but the owner will receive a printed warning

People often need to borrow money to buy expensive items and pay it back over time. Before you buy something expensive, think about the following: Do you really need it or do you just want it? Is it worth paying more money for because of interest? Interest is the extra money that you pay to banks and credit card companies for letting you borrow money. It is a percentage of the money that you borrow every year. There are different ways to borrow money, such as loans, credit cards, and lines of credit.

210. Which of the following is not one of the common forms of credit?
   A. Credit card
   B. Line of credit
   C. Installment loan
   D. Bank draft

211. What is the main idea of the passage?
   A. Credit cards are risky
   B. Credit cards are expensive
   C. Good credit is important and requires people to be responsible
   D. Credit enables you to make large purchases

212. How do banks make money by issuing credit?
   A. They charge interest on the borrowed money
   B. They are backed by government
   C. They charge a one-time fee
   D. You buy a subscription that enables you to borrow money

I asked the boy Tony, why his family moved to West Virginia from Kentucky. He explained their house had caught fire. Tony's father was walking past as I was talking to his son. The Father proudly told me, "Tony was a brave man that night."

213. How many people are engaged in conversation?
   A. One
   B. Two
   C. Three
   D. Four

The fire destroyed most of the house beyond repair. Precious memories and treasures burned up in a flash. Despite the damage and loss, the family knew they had something more important. They were grateful to survive and be together.

214. What is the main idea of the passage?
   A. Safety is what matters
   B. The family was poor
   C. The family was unprepared
   D. Extensive damage was done to the house

My brother and I pressed our noses against the window in our den as we quietly watched our neighbors unpack their van. We sat motionless like spies. Their West Virginia license plate indicated they were from out of state. We decided it was our civic duty to welcome them to Lexington Kentucky.

215. Where did the family move from?
   A. Ohio
   B. West Virginia
   C. Kentucky
   D. Lexington

HMS Bounty set sail from England in December 1787. They planned to sail to Tahiti to pick up a cargo of dragon fruit saplings and deliver them to the West Indies. The crew, under Captain Bligh, arrived in Tahiti 10 months after their departure and enjoyed the tropical island for more than 5 months. No one knows why, but on April 28, 1789, Fletcher Christian, the captain's best friend and second in charge, led a mutiny with 25 other crewmembers against Bligh. Bligh, along with 18 crewmembers still loyal to him were set adrift on a 23-foot boat in the ocean. Bligh and his men managed to reach Timor with no food, maps, or tools, thanks to their skill, courage, and luck.

216. What was Bligh's position?
   A. First mate
   B. Captain
   C. Owner
   D. Second in command

217. How long did it take the crew to mutiny?
   A. 1 year
   B. 2 years
   C. 15-18 months
   D. 22-24 months

218. How many men can fit into a 23ft boat?
   A. 15
   B. 18
   C. At least 19
   D. 25

Despite being soft-spoken, Admiral Nimitz commanded 20,000 planes, 5,000 ships, and over 2 million men. However, this did not stop journalists from writing: "the Admiral was...the despair of his public relations men; it simply was not his nature to make sweeping statements or give colorful interviews."

219. What is the main idea of the passage?
   A. Nimitz was a quiet individual
   B. The US Navy had a lot of airplanes and ships
   C. Nimitz did not like journalists
   D. Nimitz was not a good leader

Pablo Picasso's full name was Pablo Nepomuceno Crispin Crispiniano de los Remedios Cipriano de la Santisima Trinidad Ruis Picasso. He shortened it to Pablo Picasso (the first and last words) of his original long legal name. Picasso's art became legendary due to his eclectic combination of genius and talent that few could match. His work evolved throughout his life and had several distinct periods. He is famous for his role in creating the Cubism style. Cubism had three stages, Facet Cubism, Analytic Cubism, and Synthetic Cubism. The first Cubist painting was made by Picasso in 1907. It is called Les Demoiselles d'Avignon and you can see it at the Museum of Modern Art in New York. Picasso's art is still very popular and influential today.

220. What is the main idea of the passage?
   A. Picasso creation and influence on Cubism
   B. The life of Pablo Picasso
   C. Location of his work
   D. Description of the first cubist painting

221. Which is not a phase of Cubism?
   A. Facet
   B. Analytical
   C. Synthetic
   D. Block

Tailgating a vehicle is not only illegal, but also dangerous Most rear-end collisions result from drivers following too close to the car in front of them. The law states: "Drivers must maintain sufficient distance from the vehicle in front of them in order to safely stop and avoid a collision." To comply with the law, drivers should maintain a gap of at least two seconds with the vehicle ahead of them. A larger gap of three seconds should be applied when the weather is bad or visibility is low.

222. Why is it unsafe to tailgate?
   A. All rear end collisions are caused by drivers following too close
   B. It may not allow enough time to stop and avoid a collision
   C. It is against the law
   D. It is reckless

223. It can be inferred that a longer gap is needed in adverse conditions due to:
   A. People drive faster in bad weather
   B. The author is being extra cautions
   C. It is required by law
   D. Adverse conditions can make driving more difficult; the extra time provides additional stopping distance

Lake Condaha, 40 miles northeast of Portland, is not your usual destination. The site contains the remains of many aboriginal settlements. Although the buildings are gone, you can still see the round stone bases for hundreds of huts. The huts vary in size and have cutouts for doors. Rock-lined water channels and stone tools used to build *these features can still be found in the area.   The settlement flourished due to abundant fishing in the area. Locals developed sophisticated means to trap the fish by redirecting streams and lining them with stone. At internals, Aboriginals would pile rocks across the water to divert the stream into funnels to catch eels in fishing baskets.*

224. Where would this passage most likely appear?
 A.   History textbook
 B.   Postcard
 C.   Travel advertisement
 D.   Novel

225. Why is Lake Condaha an unusual destination?
 A.   It is close to a large town
 B.   It has abundant fishing
 C.   It has stone buildings
 D.   It contains remnants from many Aboriginal settlements

The bond of the sea exists between us. It holds our hearts together during periods of long separation and makes us tolerant of one another's habits. As we sailed, the lawyer lounged on the only cushion on the deck while the accountant brought out some dominoes in a fruitless attempt to pass the time. Marlow slumped against the mast with sunken cheeks and a pale face. After the Captain was satisfied that the anchor would hold, he returned to the group and lazily said a few words. We felt lethargic, fit for nothing; all we could do was stare at the sea. As the sunset, the gloom of darkness brooded over the upper reaches of the yacht and became increasingly somber with every passing minute. At last, the sun sank below the horizon. Its warmth faded as darkness hung over the crowd of men.

226. The narrator is telling the story from:
 A.   A pier
 B.   A yacht
 C.   A high vantage point
 D.   A rowboat

227. The mood of the men in the passage can be described as:
 A.   Resigned
 B.   Restless
 C.   Ecstatic
 D.   Restless

228. From the passage, it is clear that the men:
 A.   Do not get along
 B.   Have just had a fight
 C.   Anxious
 D.   Resigned to their fate

Tyrannosaurus Rex was a large and fierce dinosaur that many people think was the biggest and fastest of all predators. However, new research shows that this was not true. They were actually clumsy animals that could only run at 25 mph, which is slow compared to modern predators. They were very heavy and weighed between six to eight tons. Modern predators are fast, agile, and can change direction quickly. Tyrannosaurus Rex would have been slow at turning because of its size. But this did not matter, because its prey was also slow and clumsy. Researchers used computer models based on fossil measurements to determine the animal's characteristics.

229. When turning a Tyrannosaurus Rex would have been impeded by
   A. The length of its tail
   B. Its leg muscles
   C. Its overall size
   D. All of the above

230. To calculate size, speed, and agility what did researches use
   A. Fossil measurements
   B. Computers models using fossil measurements
   C. Fossil measurements in comparison to other animals
   D. Computer models and soft tissue analysis

231. What is the theme of the passage?
   A. It's a surprise Tyrannosaurus rex survived
   B. Tyrannosaurus' Rex's speed and agility were superior to other animals
   C. Tyrannosaurus Rex was a fierce and vicious animal
   D. Tyrannosaurs Rex is not as nimble as people once believed

The Hare had many friends among the other animals, who all said they liked her. They were all bigger, taller, stronger, and braver than her. One day, she heard the foxes coming and asked her friends for help. She thought that is what friends were for. The horse declined saying it had important work to do for the master. The bull, who had horns, replied that he had more pressing matters with his lady, while the goat was afraid his back would give out. As the foxes approached, the hare had no choice but to flee alone.

232. Why did the hare believe her friends would help?
   A. She assumed here friends would help
   B. Her friends were bigger, taller, and stronger
   C. She was popular
   D. Her friends promised to help

233. What is the moral of the story?
   A. You should always help your friends
   B. Popularity and friendship are not the same
   C. Animals aren't true friends
   D. Your friends can't be trusted

Dahlgren Hall has been a familiar landmark for drivers on the Los Angeles freeway for decades. Despite changes to the downtown landscape, the building has been a fixture since 1932. The hall is owned and operated by the city and serves as a living memorial to all Veterans.

234. Which of the following is true according to the passage?
    A. The building does not honor post WWI veterans
    B. The building will need to be renovated to match the skyline
    C. The building houses Veterans
    D. The building is a memorial

The debate on carbon trading in Australia ended last week when the Government committed to reducing national emissions. However, how the economy would manage these reductions in a carbon-constrained world is still unclear. Coal and oil have been the backbone of Australia's economic growth and created a healthy standard of living for decades. Even though Australia is seeking to reduce its emissions, other countries are not and desire these fossil fuels as a cheap source of energy. This demand will make it profitable to continue mining in the near term. New technologies like solar, wind, and geothermal will help Australia to balance its current emissions as more companies invest in these technologies. In the end, people will choose the cheapest and most profitable solution. This causes competing interesting groups to lobby the local and national government to achieve their desired outcomes. Until the government sets a mandate, fortunes and capital will rise and fall as competing technologies battle for dominance.

235. Why will fossil fuels continue to be in demand?
    A. They are plentiful and cheap
    B. We have no other option
    C. It's not possible to change energy sources
    D. Nuclear power is restricted

236. Why will fortunes rise and fall?
    A. Companies invested poorly
    B. Carbon policies will cripple the economy
    C. Fossil fuels are becoming more expensive
    D. Change is expensive, few companies will successfully adapt to the change

Many aircraft have disappeared in the middle of the ocean. One of the most famous instances is that of Amelia Earhart, an American aviator who vanished without a trace. No one knows if she crash-landed on a remote island or fell into the ocean after running out of fuel. Theories regarding her disappearance have been debated for decades. One of the more colorful stories says she was captured by the Japanese and executed as a Spy, while others claim she was successful in her trip around the world and lived out her days in suburban America. Her disappearance still captivates people's imagination and has been featured in many books, newspaper articles, and documentaries. The two most likely explanations are that she crashed on a small island or ditched the aircraft over water. Reports of distress calls being broadcast from her frequency were reported for days after her disappearance. Both the Navy and Coast Guard, who heard these signals on Howland Island, believe the calls were credible. People believe she would only have been able to broadcast for such a long period if she crashed on land. However, others believe these broadcasts are a hoax. Some believe she was forced to ditch in the ocean. If this were true, they claim her aircraft is at the bottom of the ocean in pristine condition. Her disappearance continues to fascinate investigators as the most famous missing person case.

237. What nationality was Amelia Earhart?
    A. English
    B. Australian
    C. Canadian
    D. American

238. All of the following are theories about her fate except:
    A. Crash landed on a remote island
    B. Crash landed in the ocean
    C. Crash landed at Howland Island
    D. Captured by the Japanese and executed

239. If the aircraft were found in the ocean, how would it most likely look?
    A. Unrecognizable
    B. In pristine condition
    C. Slightly damaged
    D. Severely damaged

240. Investigators are fascinated by Amelia Earhart's disappearance for all the reasons except:
    A. She was a famous female aviator
    B. The number of conflicting theories about her disappearance
    C. It remains one of the greatest unsolved mysteries
    D. She may have been captured and executed during the war

Land clearing in the Tweed Valley began in 1861, marking the start of extensive logging operations that targeted the valley's renowned Cedar trees. These ancient giants, some over 2000 years old and reaching heights of 60 meters, were prized for their length, making them highly sought after by sawmills. Cedar was in demand for its lightweight properties, rich colors, and distinctive aroma. The proximity of these trees to the river facilitated easy transportation; logs were simply floated downstream to the river's mouth and then shipped to larger cities for processing and use.

However, just nine years into this booming industry, the cedar trade experienced a rapid collapse. The relentless harvesting had rapidly depleted the stock of large trees, leading to scarcity and the industry's downfall. Tragically, the land was left *barren, as reforestation efforts were not undertaken following the cedar's extraction. This historical episode serves as a poignant reminder of the consequences of unsustainable resource exploitation.*

241. The cedar was valued for all the reasons except:
    A. Cedar is popular in furniture making
    B. Cedar has intense coloring
    C. Cedar is very tall
    D. Cedar is a lightweight wood

242. What caused the decline of the industry?
    A. Fallen trees were not replaced
    B. Trees were not growing back
    C. Trees were harvest at an unsustainable rate
    D. Cedar became less popular

We felt the metal swing on the wooden porch burn our skin as the sun beat down mercilessly. We implored Grandma to let us escape the heat and go inside, but she was adamant. Hoping for some relief from a cool breeze or a shady spot, I proposed we take a stroll in the woods. But Grandma was not to be swayed. She insisted that we sit on the porch, because that was the proper thing to do after dinner, and she was not about to break tradition.

243. What does the author imply?
    A. Grandma cooked dinner
    B. Grandma doesn't like the forest
    C. Grandma can't hear well
    D. Grandma is resistant to change

A lamb's thick coat keeps it warm during the cold winter months. The coat is sheared during summer when the temperatures rise. Once the lamb's coat is sheared it is called wool and made into yarn, which is then used to make clothes.

244. Why are lambs sheared?
    A. To prevent the animal from overheating in the summer
    B. To make yarn for clothes
    C. To prevent it from getting long
    D. To prevent it from getting dirty

Deoxyribonucleic acid, or DNA, is a strand of proteins that exist as chromosomes. These proteins contain the blueprint for physical characteristics inherited from all previous generations. There are slight variations in DNA from species to species, including plants.

245. What does the author imply?
    A. Plants are organisms
    B. All species have similar characteristics
    C. Physical traits are inherited

D. Chromosomes and DNA are the same

The Mississippi River is the lifeblood of New Orleans, giving it success and fame. The city offers a variety of attractions, from steamboat cruises and swamp tours, to historical landmarks and musical venues. And of course, there is the Jazz. Some people say that the music's beat is the pulse of the river itself.

246. According to the passage, why is New Orleans successful?
    A. The Jazz
    B. Seafood
    C. The Mississippi River
    D. Its rich history

The main character's journey is the core of the storyline, which consists of the events that shape their development. There may also be subplots that involve other, minor characters, who add depth and complexity to the storyline. Writers often intertwine the main and minor characters' stories to create a realistic plot that shows how they affect each other, mirroring real life.

247. What is the author comparing?
    A. Events and characters
    B. A realistic plot to real life
    C. Supporting and main characters
    D. Main plot vs sub plots

Culture is the shared set of behaviors that reflect the values, traditions, and history of a group of people. This does not mean that people who share a culture have to live in the same geographic area. However, it does mean that they have similar social norms.

248. People in a community will:
    A. Live together
    B. Speak a common language
    C. Celebrate the same traditions
    D. Follow the same social standards

The Humane Society is the US's largest animal protection agency. It operates at least eight shelters in each of the 50 cities it has contracts with, as well as in all unincorporated areas of the state. It also offers on-call rescue services and animal control 24 hours a day, 7 days a week.

249. Which of the following is true:
    A. The Humane Society only handles domestic animals
    B. The Humane Society provides services for some cities
    C. The Humane Society provides services for all incorporated areas
    D. Humane Society services must be scheduled in advance

American Sign Language, also known as ASL, is a conceptual language that connects concepts via syntax. In ASL, a conversation always starts with the main idea and follows with additional detail. This style is different from that of English.

250. What does the author imply?
     A. English language cannot be conceptual
     B. Every language as the same syntax
     C. ASL doesn't use syntax
     D. English does not always begin with the main idea/topic

Dolphins use a variety of sounds, such as clicks, chirps, and whistles, to communicate with each other and explore their surroundings. Scientists are still trying to decipher the meaning and purpose of these sounds, but they have made some discoveries. For example, clicks are used for echolocation, which helps dolphins hunt and navigate. Whistles seem to be the main way dolphins communicate but this requires further research. Scientists do not know yet if whistles are simple sound signals or part of a more sophisticated communication system..

251. Why are whistles significant?
     A. They indicate dolphins are human like
     B. They raise questions about the complexity of dolphin communication
     C. They are used for hunting and navigation
     D. They are not used for communication purposes

252. Which statement is true according to the passage?
     A. Dolphins are one of many species that can communicate among themselves
     B. Dolphins don't use clicks to communicate with each other
     C. Dolphins are one of the most intelligent species
     D. Dolphins frequently communicate with one another

Steve Harrow's new groundbreaking study on Rick Irwin's plays will change how future generations understand his work. Scholars had previously looked at the parts of Irwin's career in isolation, which had created arbitrary and false divisions. Harrow's work takes a holistic approach that examines Irwin's plays as a whole. This reveals a comprehensive picture of Irwin's artistic vision and contribution, enabling us to fully grasp his significance and legacy.

253. What is the main idea of the passage?
     A. Harrow overcame difficulty
     B. Harrow's work needs to be researched
     C. Harrow's study was overly complicated
     D. Harrow's study will have lasting impacts

Cells come in different shapes and sizes, depending on their function and type. For example, plant and animal cells have some notable differences. One of them is their size: plant cells are usually much larger than animal cells, sometimes up to ten times bigger. Another difference is their structure: plant cells have some organelles that animal cells lack, such as vacuoles and chloroplasts. Vacuoles are large sacs that store water and other substances, while chloroplasts are the sites of photosynthesis, where plants make their own food. These organelles give plant cells some unique abilities and characteristics that animal cells do not have.

254. The best title for this passage would be:
   A. What's the difference? Plant and Animal cells
   B. What are cells
   C. The importance of cells
   D. Why cells are different

We are facing a global catastrophe due to individuals and companies dumping trash and chemicals into ocean. The most harmful effects are felt by marine wildlife. Pollution in the water has adverse effects on animals' reproductive cycles, depletes oxygen levels, and inhibits photosynthesis in plants. Additionally, animals can become trapped, suffocate or die from digestive issues.

255. Which statement is not supported by the passage?
   A. Pollution causes harmful effects in the ocean
   B. Trash is the deadliest form of ocean pollution
   C. Both chemicals and trash are hurting the environment
   D. Companies are mostly to blame for the problem

Vintage clothing is back in style, as young adults and teenagers across the country embrace the retro vibe. They are snapping up record players, rock t-shirts, and bomber jackets from decades past, adding a touch of nostalgia to their outfits. Old trends seem to have a lasting appeal, as each generation finds new ways to appreciate and reinvent the fashion of the past.

256. What is the main idea of the passage?
   A. People are not buying new things
   B. Records are replacing CDs
   C. Younger generations don't appreciate the past
   D. Past styles are frequently popular with the current generation coming of age

Scurvy is a condition that arises from a vitamin C deficiency, leading to symptoms like weakness, gum disease, and skin hemorrhages. The disease mainly occurred during long ocean voyages, as it was challenging to keep fresh food from spoiling. A common symptom was extreme reactions to sensory stimuli. It was not unheard of for a loud sound or a bite of fruit to kill a scurvy sailor due to the sensory shock.

257. Which of the following does the passage imply?
    A. Fresh fruit is a cure for the disease
    B. Affected sailors were at risk of other genetic mutations
    C. Affected sailors could easily die
    D. Affected sailors had an increased risk of committing suicide

A person's activity level can affect their risk of developing chronic diseases, such as cancer, diabetes, or heart disease. According to a recent study, the average person spends more than half of their day sitting, which can have negative consequences for their health. Regular exercise, on the other hand, is a key factor in enhancing one's well-being. Exercise can help prevent or manage various health conditions, improve mood and energy levels, and promote longevity.

258. What does the passage imply?
    A. Exercise counteracts sedentary behavior
    B. Exercise might not be enough to improve your health
    C. Sedentary behavior causes cancer
    D. Exercise increases your chances of being healthy

The Romantic Era sparked a revival in reading that inspired millions of people to see the world in new ways, using their imagination and emotion to connect with the writers' visions. Writers used symbols to convey their thoughts and feelings in creative ways. They experimented with different forms and styles of expression, exploring themes such as nature, emotion, imagination, and individuality.

259. What was the Romantic Era?
    A. A religious movement
    B. Literary period
    C. Cultural revolution
    D. A minor footnote in history

Tsunamis are massive waves that are caused by underwater landslides, usually triggered by an underwater earthquake. The word comes from Japan and means "harbor wave", because these waves often inflict severe damage on coastal communities. Tsunamis can travel at high speeds across the ocean, reaching heights of tens of meters and carrying enormous amounts of energy. When they reach the shore, they can destroy buildings, bridges, roads, and lives.

260. What is the best title for this passage?
    A. What is a Tsunami
    B. Natural disasters in Japan
    C. Origin of Japanese words
    D. Tsunami effects

One of the main reasons why people deliberately set structures on fire is to commit insurance fraud. They try to collect money from insurance companies by claiming that their property was destroyed in an accident. These people are not pyromaniacs, who are people who have a psychological disorder that makes them obsessed with fire and derive pleasure from setting things on fire. Another common reason why people set structures on fire is to seek revenge.

261. What is a pyromaniac?
    A. A person who sets buildings on fire
    B. A person seeking revenge
    C. A person seeking psychological satisfaction from causing a fire
    D. A person who commits insurance fraud

Thomas Edison is one of the most famous inventors in history. He invented many things that changed the world, such as the light bulb and motion photography. However, he also had many failures in his career. One of his most notorious failures was his attempt to find a better way to mine ore. Despite his tenacious effort, he was unable to develop a successful solution.

262. What is the meaning of Tenacious in context of the passage?
    A. Angry
    B. Persistent
    C. Lazy
    D. Lethargic

Parts of Alaska experience extreme variations in daylight due to its northern latitude. Most of the state lies within the Arctic Circle, a region that has continuous daylight in the summer and continuous darkness in the winter. Depending on the location and season, some parts of Alaska may not see the sun for months, while others may enjoy the midnight sun.

263. What can be inferred from the passage?
    A. All of Alaska experiences unending darkness
    B. All of Alaska experiences long hours of daylight in the summer
    C. Regions south of the arctic circle experience both darkness and daylight every day
    D. Regions south of the arctic circle experience both unending daylight and darkness

Water conservation is increasingly becoming more important as drought affects many regions. Plants have varying water needs, depending on their type and environment. Homeowners can save water by choosing plants that are drought-tolerant and require less watering. They can also water their plants during the coolest times of the day, such as early morning or evening, to reduce evaporation and water loss.

264. When should plants be watered?
    A. At 1200, noon when the sun is hottest
    B. At 0600, when the sun is just beginning to rise
    C. At 1000, when the day is beginning to warm
    D. At 1500, just after the hottest part of the day

Experts suggest that people looking to lose weight should lower their calories and exercise regularly. However, these should not be taken to extremes as too much exercise and too few calories can have adverse health effects. Caloric intake should never drop below 1200 and individuals should exercise 4-5 times a week for 30 minutes.

265. What is the best title for the passage?
    A. How to lose weight in a healthy manner
    B. The dangers of dieting
    C. Caloric recommendations for to lose weight
    D. How to avoid injury

Cell phones are indispensable in our lives, but they also have a downside A recent study found that drivers who talk on the phone performed 40% worse than drunk drivers. Researchers found that even the use of hands-free devices still impaired the driver's ability.

266. Which statement does the author most likely believe?
    A. It is not dangerous to talk on the phone while driving
    B. Hands free devices make it safe to talk on the phone and drive
    C. When driving you should not talk on the phone
    D. Talking on phone while driving is safer than drunk driving

267. What is the main idea of the passage?
    A. Drunk driving is less dangerous than driving while talking on the phone
    B. The benefits of hands-free driving
    C. The dangerous of driving while talking on the phone
    D. Alternative methods to talking on the phone while driving

Carjacking's have increased in the last decade, despite efforts to prevent them. You can reduce the risk of being a victim of a carjacking by following some simple tips. Always walk with someone to your car, and keep it locked and windows up when you drive. Avoid isolated roads and stick to busy ones with other cars around.

268. What is the best title for the passage?
    A. Carjacking Victim Prevention
    B. The rise of carjacking's
    C. Driving safely
    D. What to do in a carjacking

269. Which of the following statements does the author most likely believe?
    A. It's impossible to prevent carjacking's
    B. Carjacking's mostly happen at night
    C. Carjacking's don't occur during the day
    D. Simple preventive measures can reduce your risk of being carjacked

Blood flows from your heart's left atrium to the left ventricle through the mitral valve. This valve plays a crucial role by controlling circulation throughout the body and is a powerful circulatory muscle. If your heart were exposed, the mitral valve could shoot blood as high as five feet.

270. What is the author's purpose?
- A. Describe the circulatory system
- B. Inform readers of heart defects
- C. Inform readers of the values importance
- D. Describe what happens when the heart is cut open

Opera is a musical art form that originated in Europe. It uses a musical ensemble to express emotions and tell a story. It is often accompanied with a vocalist who sings, rather than speaks. Musical theater, in contrast, relies on an actor's performance and less so on their vocal ability or musical accompaniment. Drama on the other hand primarily uses costumes, scenery, and acting to tell a story.

271. Which of the following is implied by the passage?
- A. Opera developed under the influence of musical theater
- B. Opera is sung and accompanied by a musical element
- C. Opera costs less to produce
- D. Opera is popular in Europe

272. According to the passage, which of the following is true
- A. People prefer opera to musical theater
- B. Musical theater relies on a symphony
- C. In opera vocal elements are not spoken
- D. Opera doesn't have anything in common with theater

Dolphins have a long history of saving drowning sailors, dating back to the Roman times. They are known as the friendliest creatures in the sea. Humans often think they are the most intelligent species on the planet, but dolphins might challenge that assumption. Dolphins care for their sick, injured, pregnant, and young, just like humans do. Some have proposed that dolphins have a unique language that we have yet to decipher, however everyone agrees that they are more complex than we previously imagined.. It's possible that dolphins are even more intelligent than humans.

273. Which of the following statements is true?
- A. Dolphins are less intelligent than previously thought
- B. Dolphins are the strongest sea creatures
- C. Dolphins don't take care of each other
- D. Dolphins have a reputation for being friendly

274. What can be inferred from the passage?
- A. Dolphins have social traits that are like humans
- B. Dolphins are abundant in many areas of the ocean
- C. Dolphins don't communicate via sound
- D. Dolphins in the future will be able to communicate with humans

The Estonia ferry disaster was a terrible tragedy that should never have happened. The ship was well maintained, had passed all safety checks, and had enough lifeboats for everyone. But only a few hours after leaving port the ship rolled over in a storm and sank. It was too dark and sank too fast for most people to escape, and many who did froze to death in the water. Only 139 out of 900 people survived, mostly young and fit men.

275. What can be inferred from the passage?
    A. Lifesaving equipment did not function properly
    B. Design defects caused the vessel to sink
    C. Many victims were trapped inside the vessel
    D. The crew was incompetent

Soil erosion is a serious problem for American farmland. It started when the settlers cleared the grasslands for farming in the 18th century. Despite conservation efforts, erosion has accelerated due to increased demand on the land. Wind and water wash away the soil and make it less fertile. If not addressed, soil erosion in combination with pollution will cause a national resource emergency.

276. Soil erosion:
    A. Has caused humans to increase demands on land production
    B. Is worsening and could be a national emergency
    C. Is hardly noticeable
    D. Has decreased due to conservation efforts

Language has steadily declined over the years. This is not because of bad writers, but because of economic and political factors. A person may drink excessively because they view themselves as a failure. However, the more they drink, the more they fail. The same is happening with language. Language is becoming less clear and more clumsy because of slang and "fake words". People use these words and they become part of the language.

277. What statement would the author most likely agree with?
    A. Failure generally results in more failure and can cause a downward spiral
    B. Language has eroded due to the influence of certain writers
    C. Economic and political failings cause language to decline
    D. People's excessive drinking has caused language to decline

Wildlife conservation is as important as natural resource conservation. When a nation squanders its natural resources, they become lost for generations, but when wildlife is wasted, it is gone forever. People mistakenly believe nature has abundant resources that can always be replenished. This is why poachers frequently get away with killing, while legal hunters are blamed for destroying wildlife. We all have a shared interest in conserving wildlife.

278. Which of the following is implied?
    A. Conservation conflicts with human development
    B. Poachers must be punished
    C. Once loss, wildlife can't be replaced
    D. People are unaware of conservation efforts

Though many seeds fall on the ground, few plants actually grow. The seeds compete for light and water, and fight with other plants for survival. Many plants die in the process. The same happens with animals. Even without humans, millions of animals die during adolescence. Most die from natural causes and illness. The law of survival is constant for all species, only the strongest survive.

279. What is the main point of the passage?
    A. Individuals in a population are in competition with one another
    B. In the struggle to survive, the most fit survive
    C. Human influence destroys natures balance
    D. Different generations have the same survival rates

Drug addiction is a topic that has many literature sources, but not much clarity. But, even with more content, understanding of the problem remains elusive. Addiction, or dependence as it is often called, is a controversial and debated issue. Some people see it as a disease, others as a choice. The terms used to describe drug dependence are vague and biased. Even the official definition of a drug by the World Health Organization is too wide, is too broad since a drug is defined as anything that modifies an organism's functions. This could describe anything from aspirin to alcohol.

280. What does the author imply with the term "dependence" in context of drugs?
    A. The term is more accurate than addiction
    B. The term is under utilized
    C. The term is controversial
    D. The word has not always been the preferred term in the context of drugs

281. Which of the following can be inferred?
    A. It is fashionable to write about addiction
    B. Not everything written on drugs adds to our understanding
    C. There is too much literature on drugs
    D. Writing would improve if there was better understanding

Crowds line up and cheer for the explorer upon their return. Many feel proud of the achievement on behalf of the country. Some even go so far as to claim the feather in their own cap. However, how many in the crowd were there when the expedition was short on supplies, or on the brink of collapse. How many were there when life hung in the balance. When times are desperate, leaders often find themselves alone in overcoming the greatest of difficulties.

282. What is the phrase "feather in their own cap" referring to?
    A. Willingness to take unearned credit
    B. Receiving a reward for investing
    C. A means to express joy
    D. A way to express success

Amundsen and Columbus were adventurous explorers who never gave up on their goals. Amundsen sailed across the Arctic Ocean by himself on a small yacht when he was only 15. He followed a route that others had failed at navigating for over 400 years. He had trouble finding money, supporters, and equipment before this journey. In fact, no one noticed him until he finished his journey. Columbus faced similar difficulties in getting support, funds, and finding a crew for his voyage. Both explorers left on their journeys without fanfare or hopes of surviving like many before them.

283. Amundsen and Columbus shared all the following except:
    A. Were explorers
    B. Sailed alone
    C. Were not initially supported
    D. Had difficulties prior to beginning their journeys

The US in the 1920s would be a huge contrast to the vision of the Declaration of Independence signers. How would they feel about inventions like the car, the electric light, or the airplane? Would they be impressed or scared? They most certainly would be shocked by the ban on alcohol. The German Empire they fought against would be no more. Would they be proud or disappointed by the Republic they founded? The ban on alcohol would certainly lead them to believe there was a breakdown in the principles of government they had fought to create.

284. What is the purpose of the passage?
    A. Introduce constitutional amendments
    B. Summarize social and political changes between 1776 and 1920
    C. Provide a short discussion on political history
    D. Share the authors feelings towards Prohibition

A sanctuary is not just a place where nature is free and human activity is limited. It is also a place where humans can help nature when needed. Humans can do more than just watch. Nature can benefit from activities such as pest and parasite eradication in addition to cures for diseases that occasionally wipe out entire populations of rabbits. Which if were to occur would cause animals, like foxes, to starve. However, intervention should not be the norm, as Nature has a way of balancing itself.

285. What does the author imply about the first definition of a sanctuary?
    A. It's idealistic
    B. It's wrong
    C. It's unhelpful
    D. It's correct

286. Which statement by the author weakened their case for intervention?
   A. Parasites are a result of human activity
   B. Elimination of pests involves insecticides which are harmful to the environment
   C. Nature naturally balances itself
   D. Elimination of a specifics can have unattended consequences

What some people call pleasure, others call an effort to destroy consciousness. Just because one can skip work to have fun does not mean one should. Humans need more than leisure and comfort; they also need creative works and solitude. Happiness is not something you can get from relaxing, drinking beer, or playing poker. It is something you find in life itself.

287. What does the author imply about humans?
   A. People who seek pleasure are less human
   B. Technology is alienating humans
   C. Humans have needs beyond comfort
   D. Humans are searching for the meaning of life

288. What would the author most likely say about a person playing poker?
   A. They are trying to avoid thinking
   B. They are searching for true pleasure
   C. It is something people should avoid
   D. It is a vice

NASA's Pioneer spacecraft proved that Venus is extremely hot due to the greenhouse effect from the carbon dioxide in the atmosphere. The greenhouse effect causes surface heating because reflected energy is unable to escape the atmosphere. Earth and Venus both have thin air, but Earth's atmosphere is 4% carbon dioxide while Venus' is 90% carbon dioxide. By studying Venus, we can learn how carbon dioxide affects our own atmosphere.

289. What is true regarding the atmosphere of Venus?
   A. It is thinner than Earth's
   B. It traps less heat
   C. It blocks the suns dangerous rays
   D. It contains more carbon dioxide than Earth's

290. What can be inferred from the passage?
   A. There is litter difference between the atmosphere of Venus and Earth
   B. The more carbon dioxide there is in the atmosphere the warmer it tends to be
   C. Earth's atmosphere is mostly carbon dioxide
   D. Lack of atmosphere causes high surface temperatures on Venus

The brain is a complex organ that has many functions. The hippocampus, which is in the front of the brain, helps us remember things. It turns what we see, hear, smell, taste, and touch into images with the help of neurons. These images are stored in short-term memory, but they don't last long. Some of them are moved to long-term memory, which is in the cerebral cortex. Scientists believe that this happens when we sleep, but they don't know how exactly.

291. What is the passage about?
    A. How we can improve our memory
    B. Why short-term memory fades
    C. How the brain processes and stores information
    D. The importance of neurons in memory

292. Which of the following is true according to the passage?
    A. Scientists don't know how information is transferred between short and long-term memory
    B. Scientists know how information is transferred between short and long-term memory
    C. Scientists understand how memory fades
    D. Scientists agree on how the brain works

Readers are attracted to stories involving people who have extraordinary abilities. One famous example is that of Vera Petrova who was able to perceive information through touch, some even said she could see through walls. Her ability attracted the interest of a research institute who conduct a series of tests. They discovered that except for when her fingers were wet, that she was able perceive information through her fingers no matter the thickness or type of material. They determined that even when blindfolded, she could see through her fingers.

293. When does Vera lose the ability to perceive through her skin?
    A. When the object is hidden
    B. When she is blindfolded
    C. When her fingers are wet
    D. When she is being tested

294. Which of the following is true according to the passage:
    A. The research institute is not interested in Vera
    B. Vera loses her ability when she is blindfolded
    C. The institute puts together a list of experts to conduct the study
    D. Vera can perceive objects when blindfolded

The Bermuda Triangle has a long and storied history. Since 1945, more than 100 planes and ships have been reported as missing in the area with thousands of lives lost. To date, neither wreckage nor bodies from these incidents ever have been found. Some vessels have disappeared under unusual circumstances such as a spinning compass or unusual sky, while others disappeared in mid conversation while on the radio.

295. What can be inferred from the passage?
    A. Disappearances first started being recorded in 1945
    B. Some wreckage has been found in the Bermuda Triangle
    C. The percentage of lost ships and aircraft is no different than other parts of the world
    D. The Bermuda triangle has bad weather

296. What is the main idea of the passage?
    A. Why disappearances occur in the Bermuda Triangle
    B. Note the frequency of disappearances in the Bermuda Triangle
    C. Inform about disappearances in the Bermuda Triangle
    D. Talk about the Bermuda Triangle's weather conditions

The Weights and Measurement Commission regularly conducts price inspections to ensure companies are selling what they advertise. An inspector will usually pick 15 items at random for a price check. If the price of the item is different at checkout than what is shown on the shelf the store will receive a violation notice. If a store receives too many violations, the case may be turned over to the District Attorney's office for further prosecution.

297. Which of the following is true according to the passage?
    A. Inspectors usually find price errors for at least one of the 15 items
    B. Violations are automatically turned over to the District Attorney
    C. Items costing less than the listed price are free
    D. A violation occurs when the charged price does not match the listed price

The Tri-State Fire Department's mission is to safeguard the lives, property, and environment of the County's unincorporated areas. The department provides prompt and lifesaving services to about 20,000 residents in a cost-effective manner. The budget for the current fiscal year allows the department to reorganize and create new positions for community representatives.

298. Which of the following is true according to the passage?
    A. The fire department is responsible for the unincorporated area of the county
    B. The fire department is tasked with only protecting lives
    C. The fire department is having budget issues
    D. The fire department has jurisdiction over other areas in the county

An Ombudsman's job is to advocate for Children who live in group homes. They work independently from the agencies that place the children into foster homes. Children can call their Ombudsman when they have problems or need help in resolving a dispute. These conversations are kept strictly confidential.

299. Which of the following is true regarding Ombudsman?
    A. Anonymous communications to the Ombudsman are not acted upon
    B. Ombudsman are a resource children can contact when in need
    C. Foster agencies are responsible for assigning Ombudsman
    D. Ombudsman initiate an investigation when they receive a complaint

A "certified Farmers" Market requires its sellers to deliver their products directly from a farm that is located within the county's jurisdiction. To retain this certification County inspectors will periodically visit each participating farm to verify what crops are being grown. Inspectors will occasionally check the market to ensure sellers are selling what they grow.

300. Which statement is correct?
    A. Where the inspection occurs depends on what the farmer grows
    B. Produce sold at a Farmers Market is of a higher quality
    C. Farmers are able to purchase and resell other items not produced on their farm
    D. The inspector's job is to ensure sellers are meet the certification requirements.

Answer Key

1. C

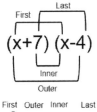

First   Outer   Inner   Last

$$x^2-4x+7x-28$$

$$x^2+3x-28$$

2. C

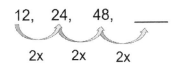

3. D

$$A = \frac{B \times 15}{C}$$

$$5 = \frac{14 \times 15}{C}$$

$$5C = 210$$

$$C = 42$$

4. B

```
      0.215
6 ) 1.29
    12
     9
     6
    30
    30
     0
```

5. A

$$\frac{15}{100}(80) =$$
$$= \frac{1200}{100}$$
$$= 12$$

6. B

$$\frac{x}{6} = \frac{3x}{6} - \frac{8}{6}$$
$$x = 3x - 8$$
$$-2x = -8$$
$$x = 4$$

7. C

Solve for A
$$6A = B - 6$$
$$A = \frac{B - 6}{6}$$
$$A = \frac{B}{6} - 1$$

If A is greater than −1, then B will be positive

8. C

$$
\begin{array}{r}
14 \\
25\,)\,\overline{350} \\
\underline{25} \\
100 \\
\underline{100}
\end{array}
$$

9. A

We are looking for equations that have y-intercepts of −2 and 5. From the graph we can see that line which has a y-intercept of −2 has a slope of 2. The equation for a line is y=mx+b. *b* is the y-intercept and *m* is the slope. The only option which has m=2 and b=-2 is option A.

10. B

$$\frac{x}{72 - x} = \frac{2}{7}$$
$$7x = 2(72 - x)$$
$$7x = 144 - 2x$$
$$9x = 144$$
$$x = 16$$

11. **B**

$$
\begin{array}{r}
10.5 \\
35\overline{)\,367.5} \\
35 \\
\hline
175 \\
175 \\
\hline
0
\end{array}
$$

12. **C**

$$= \frac{10}{3} \times \frac{3}{2}$$
$$= \frac{30}{6}$$
$$= 5$$

13. **C**

$$9 \times 12 = 108$$

14. **A**

$$6xy - (3xy - 3x^2)$$
$$= 6xy - 3xy + 3x^2$$
$$= 3xy + 3x^2$$

15. **B**

$$\frac{\text{spade}}{\text{all cards in deck}}$$
$$= \frac{4}{4 + 3 + 7 + 10}$$
$$= \frac{4}{24}$$
$$= \frac{1}{6}$$

16. **A**

$$A : 8(10) = 80$$
$$B : 3(25) = 75$$
$$C : \quad 79 = 79$$
$$D : 15(5) = 75$$

17. B

$$
\begin{array}{r}
256 \\
\times \quad 2 \\
\hline
512
\end{array}
$$

The sum of the decimal places for the original products is three. Therefore, move the decimal point three places to the left to get **0.512**

18. A

$$\frac{70}{100}(800) =$$

$$= \frac{56000}{100}$$

$$= 560$$

19. D

Calculate the price of 1 turkey with the coupon.

$$10 \times \frac{88}{100} = 8.8$$

Sum the discounted and regular price turkeys:

$$8.8 + 10 = 18.80$$

20. C

$$
\begin{array}{r}
126.7 \\
- \quad 14.65 \\
\hline
112.05 \\
+ \quad 4.389 \\
\hline
116.439
\end{array}
$$

Rounding to the nearest hundredth yields: **116.44**

21. D

$$A : (-2)^2 + 3(-2) - 7 = 4 - 6 - 7 = -9$$
$$B : (-2)^2 - 2(-2) + 9 = 4 + 4 + 9 = 17$$
$$C : (-2)^2 + 7(-2) - 14 = 4 - 14 - 14 = -24$$
$$D : (-2)^2 - 6(-2) + 9 = 4 + 12 + 9 = 25$$

22. A

$$\frac{4}{x} + \frac{2}{6} = \frac{5}{x}$$

$$\frac{24}{6x} + \frac{2x}{6x} = \frac{30}{6x}$$
$$24 + 2x = 30$$
$$2x = 6$$
$$x = 3$$

23. A

	Current Age	Age -5
Jeremy	T+12	T+12-5 T+7
Tim	T	T-5

Five years ago, the sum of their ages was 28
$$T + 7 + T - 5 = 28$$
$$2T + 2 = 28$$
$$2T = 26$$
$$T = 13$$

24. C

$$\frac{new - old}{old} =$$
$$= \frac{2.8 - 2.5}{2.50}$$
$$= \frac{0.3}{2.5}$$

Divide to calculate the percentage:

$$\begin{array}{r} 0.12 \\ 25\overline{)3.00} \\ \underline{25} \\ 9 \\ \underline{5} \\ 50 \\ \underline{50} \\ 0 \end{array}$$

25. D

$$\frac{5 \times 8}{6 \times 9} =$$
$$= \frac{40}{54}$$
$$= \frac{20}{27}$$

26. A

1 hour is equivalent to 60 minutes. In 4 hours, he'll have run 40 miles

27. C

$$2(x + 7) - 3(2x - 4) = -18$$
$$2x + 14 - 6x + 12 = -18$$
$$-4x + 26 = -18$$
$$-4x = -44$$
$$x = 11$$

28. C

$$8(5.12) + 0.5(5.12) =$$
$$= 40.96 + 2.56$$
$$= 43.52$$

29. B

$$\frac{35}{100}\, x = 14$$
$$35x = 1400$$
$$x = 40$$

30. D

Options A, B, and C can immediately be ruled out since the value in the numerator is less than half of the denominator. Option D is the only choice which has a numerator that is more than half of the denominator.

$$A : 0.29$$
$$B : 0.46$$
$$C : 0.44$$
$$D : 0.57$$

31. A

There is an equal number of pizza's being order as there are friends. Therefore, each person pays for one pizza.

32. A

$$3, \quad 3, \quad 6, \quad 18, \quad 72, \quad \underline{}$$

x1   x2   x3   x4   x5

33. C

$$\frac{6}{3486} = \frac{7}{x}$$
$$6x = 7(3486)$$
$$6x = 24402$$
$$x = 4067$$

34. B

We can quickly estimate the correct answer B because 108 is nearly half of 240.

$$\frac{45}{100} \, 240 = x$$
$$45(240) = 100x$$
$$10800 = 100x$$
$$x = 108$$

35. A

The equation of a line is y=mx+b , where *b* is the y-intercept and *m* is the slope. The line has a y-intercept of –2 and a slope of 2.

36. D

$$
\begin{array}{r}
388 \\
\times \quad 55 \\
\hline
1940 \\
1940 \\
\hline
2134.0
\end{array}
$$

37. A

$$\frac{x^2 - y^2}{x - y} =$$
$$= \frac{(x+y)(x-y)}{(x-y)}$$
$$= x + y$$

38. B

$$450(30) = 13500$$

39. B

$$\frac{6}{12} + \frac{2}{12} + \frac{1}{12} = \frac{6+2+1}{12} = \frac{9}{12} = \frac{3}{4}$$

40. B

$$1, \quad 4, \quad 9, \quad 16, \quad 25, \quad \underline{\quad\quad}$$
$$\uparrow \quad \uparrow \quad \uparrow \quad \uparrow \quad \uparrow \quad \uparrow$$
$$1^2, \quad 2^2, \quad 3^2, \quad 4^2, \quad 5^2, \quad 6^2$$

41. D

$$\frac{30000}{100} \times 80 = 300 \times 80 = 24000$$

42. D

$$\frac{41}{100} 1400 = x$$
$$41(1400) = 100x$$
$$57400 = 100x$$
$$574 = x$$

43. A

$$2\sqrt{8} + 6\sqrt{2} =$$
$$= 2\sqrt{4 \times 2} + 6\sqrt{2}$$
$$= 2(2)\sqrt{2} + 6\sqrt{2}$$
$$= 4\sqrt{2} + 6\sqrt{2}$$
$$= 10\sqrt{2}$$

44. C

$$-12x - 2(x+9) = 5(x+4)$$
$$-12x - 2x - 18 = 5x + 20$$
$$-14x - 18 = 5x + 20$$
$$-19x = 38$$
$$x = -2$$

45. C

$$\frac{15}{100} x = 18$$
$$15x = 18(100)$$
$$15x = 1800$$
$$x = 120$$

46. C

Since 80% of the money was spent, 20% remains. Therefore:

$$\frac{20}{100}\,140 = x$$
$$20(140) = 100x$$
$$2800 = 100x$$
$$x = 28$$

47. B

$$\frac{3}{4} - \frac{5x}{4} = \frac{108}{24}$$
$$\frac{3}{4} - \frac{5x}{4} = \frac{18}{4}$$
$$3 - 5x = 18$$
$$-5x = 15$$
$$x = -3$$

48. A

$$11.40(40) + 17.1(6) =$$
$$= 456 + 102.6$$
$$= 558.60$$

49. B

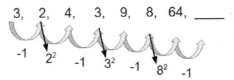

50. C

The fastest way to solve this problem is to determine which two parentheses have a value that multiplies to positive 9.

$$-3(-3) = 9$$

51. D

$$\frac{x^2 - x - 6}{x^2 - 2x - 8} =$$
$$= \frac{(x - 3)(x + 2)}{(x - 4)(x + 2)}$$
$$= \frac{x - 3}{x - 4}$$

52. D

	Current Age	Age +6
Sarah	x+28	x+34
Vivian	x	x+6

In six years, Sarah will be three times as old as Vivian. We can set up our equation as follows to solve for x:

$$x + 34 = 3(x + 6)$$
$$x + 34 = 3x + 18$$
$$16 = 2x$$
$$x = 8$$

Vivian is 8 years old, however the question is asking for Sarah's age:

$$8 + 28 = 36$$

53. B

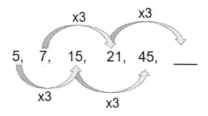

54. C

$$\frac{68}{100}600 = x$$

$$68(600) = 100x$$
$$x = 408$$

55. D

$$\frac{5}{9}(2x - 7) = x$$

$$5(2x - 7) = 9x$$
$$10x - 35 = 9x$$
$$x = 35$$

56. A

$$-9(x + 3) + 12 = -3(2x + 5) - 3x$$
$$-9x - 27 + 12 = -6x - 15 - 3x$$
$$-9x - 15 = -9x - 15$$

Since the equation is the same on both sides, it will have infinitely man solutions.

57. B

First, simplify the expression:
$$2(x^2 - 3x - 28)$$
Options B and C multiply to –28, but only B sums to –3.

58. A

P	Parenthesis
E	Exponents
M	Multiplication or Division
D	Left to Right
A	Addition or Subtraction
S	Left to Right

$$26 - 7(3 + 5) \div 4 + 2 =$$
$$= 26 - 7(8) \div 4 + 2$$
$$= 26 - 56 \div 4 + 2$$
$$= 26 - 14 + 2$$
$$= 14$$

59. C

Determine the profit per a card
$$30 - 18 = 12$$
Divide the overhead costs by the profit on each card.
$$\frac{6000}{0.12} = 50000$$

60. B

$$\frac{70}{100}\,220 = 100x$$
$$70(220) = 100x$$
$$15400 = 100x$$
$$154 = x$$

61. D

$$\frac{3}{9} + \frac{4}{6} =$$
$$= \frac{6}{18} + \frac{12}{18}$$
$$= \frac{6 + 12}{18}$$
$$= \frac{18}{18}$$
$$= 1$$

62. A

P	Parenthesis
E	Exponents
M	Multiplication or Division
D	Left to Right
A	Addition or Subtraction
S	Left to Right

$$2 - 8 \div (2^2 \div 2) =$$
$$= 2 - 8 \div (16 \div 2)$$
$$= 2 - 8 \div 8$$
$$= 2 - 1$$
$$= 1$$

63. A

$$\frac{15}{2} = \frac{750}{x}$$
$$15x = 1500$$
$$x = 100$$

64. B

-22   -22   -22

178,   156,   75,   56,   28, _____

65. B

$$
\begin{array}{r}
364.74 \\
5\,)\,\overline{1823.70} \\
\underline{15} \\
32 \\
\underline{30} \\
23 \\
\underline{20} \\
37 \\
\underline{35} \\
20 \\
\underline{20}
\end{array}
$$

66. D

$$\frac{x}{2} + \frac{x}{6} = 4$$
$$\frac{3x}{6} + \frac{x}{6} = 4$$
$$3x + x = 4(6)$$
$$4x = 24$$
$$x = 6$$

67. D

First, calculate the total number of hours worked by the 14-person team:
$$14(156) = 2184$$
Divide the total number of hours by 13
$$\frac{2184}{13} = 168$$

68. B

The equation for a parabola is:

$c=ah^2+k$

$b=-2ah$

$$ax^2+bx+c$$

The vertex of the parabola is (h,k). In this example a=1. For speed we can solve for b:
$$b = -2ah$$
$$= -2(1)(6.5)$$
$$= -13$$
Only option B has a b value of -13

69. D

$$3^5 3^2 + 3^0 =$$
$$= 3^{5+2} + 1$$
$$= 3^7 + 1$$
$$= 2187 + 1$$
$$= 2188$$

70. C

We can recreate the original shape below from the information in the text.

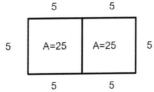

The sum of the outer lengths of the rectangle is 30.

71. C

$$\begin{array}{r} 17 \\ \times \quad 17 \\ \hline 119 \\ + \, 170 \\ \hline 289 \end{array}$$

72. A

$$\sqrt{3}(5\sqrt{3} - \sqrt{12} + \sqrt{10}) =$$
$$= \sqrt{3}(5\sqrt{3} - \sqrt{4 \times 3} + \sqrt{10})$$
$$= \sqrt{3}(5\sqrt{3} - 2\sqrt{3} + \sqrt{10})$$
$$= 5\sqrt{3}\sqrt{3} - 2\sqrt{3}\sqrt{3} + \sqrt{10}\sqrt{3}$$
$$= 5(3) - 2(6) + \sqrt{30}$$
$$= 15 - 6 + \sqrt{30}$$
$$= 9 + \sqrt{30}$$

73. B

$$\text{Mike Types} \quad = 3 \times \text{Chris}$$

Together they can type
$$\begin{aligned} \text{Mike} + \text{Chris} &= 24 \\ 3\text{Chris} + \text{Chris} &= 24 \\ 4\text{Chris} &= 24 \\ \text{Chris} &= 6 \end{aligned}$$
Therefore, Mike can type:

$$\text{Mike} = 3\text{Chris} = 3(6) = 18$$

If Chris times as fast as Mike then:
$$18 + 18 = 36$$

74. A

$$x^2 + 12x + 36 =$$
$$= (x + 6)(x + 6)$$

$$x + 6 = 0$$
$$x = -6$$

75. A

$$\begin{array}{ll} \text{Start} & = 10 \\ \text{1 hour} & = 20 \\ \text{2 hour} & = 40 \\ \text{3 hour} & = 80 \\ \text{4 hour} & = 160 \\ \text{5 hour} & = 320 \end{array}$$

76. B

$$4\frac{1}{5} + 2\frac{1}{5} + 3\frac{3}{10} =$$
$$= \frac{21}{5} + \frac{11}{5} + \frac{33}{10}$$
$$= \frac{42}{10} + \frac{22}{10} + \frac{33}{10}$$
$$= \frac{42 + 22 + 33}{10}$$
$$= \frac{97}{10}$$
$$= 9\frac{7}{10}$$

77. A

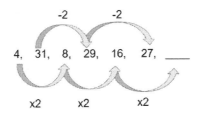

4,   31,   8,   29,   16,   27,   _____

78. C

$$\frac{18}{100}\,250 = x$$
$$18(250) = 100x$$
$$4500 = 100x$$
$$x = 45$$

79. B

$$\frac{4}{50} = \frac{x}{100}$$
$$50x = 4(100)$$
$$50x = 400$$
$$x = 8$$

80. A

$$(a-b)(a^2+ab+b^2)+a^3+b^3 \quad =$$
$$= -a^2b - ab^2 - b^3 + a^3 + a^2b + ab^2 + a^3 + b^3$$
$$= a^3 + a^3$$
$$= 2a^3$$

81. D

The fastest way to solve this problem is to determine which two parentheses have a value that multiplies to –2.

$$2(-1) = -2$$

82. C

$$\frac{x-5}{3} = \frac{x-3}{5}$$
$$5(x-5) \quad = 3(x-3)$$
$$5x - 25 \quad = 3x - 9$$
$$2x \quad = 16$$
$$x \quad = 8$$

83. B

$$\frac{5 \times 7}{8 \times 7} = \frac{35}{56}$$

84. B

$$\frac{3}{8} \times \frac{4}{6} =$$
$$= \frac{3 \times 4}{8 \times 6}$$
$$= \frac{12}{48}$$
$$= \frac{1}{4}$$

85. B

Calculate the cost of the tires without tax:

$$7(4)(68) = 1904$$

Add in the cost of the tax

$$\frac{1904(108)}{100} =$$
$$= 19.04(108)$$
$$= 2056.32$$

86. A

$$3(4x + 6)(x - 9) =$$
$$= (12x + 18)(x - 9)$$
$$= 12x^2 - 108x + 18x - 162$$
$$= 12x^2 - 90x - 162$$

87. D

$$\frac{3}{4}(x + 3) = 9$$
$$3(x + 3) = 36$$
$$3x + 9 = 36$$
$$3x = 27$$
$$x = 9$$

88. B

$$8\sqrt{28} - 3\sqrt{7} =$$
$$= 8\sqrt{7 \times 4} - 3\sqrt{7}$$
$$= 8(2)\sqrt{7} - 3\sqrt{7}$$
$$= 16\sqrt{7} - 3\sqrt{7}$$
$$= 13\sqrt{7}$$

89. C

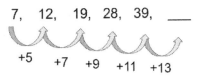

90. A

$$\begin{array}{r}
0.240 \\
\times \quad 9.9 \\
\hline
2160 \\
+ \ 21600 \\
\hline
2.3760
\end{array}$$

91. C

$$-3 \times -3 \times -3 = -27$$

92. D

$$\frac{15}{5} = \frac{6}{x}$$
$$15x = 6(5)$$
$$15x = 30$$
$$x = 2$$

93. D

First, solve for w:

$$6w + 4 = 8w$$
$$4 = 2w$$
$$w = 2$$

Plug the value of w above into 4w and solve:

$$4(2) = 8$$

94. B

$$\begin{array}{r} 3a + b = 10 \\ + \quad -4a - 2b = 2 \\ \hline -a - b = 12 \\ b = -12 - a \end{array}$$

Plug the value of b into the top equation
$$3a - 12 - 1 = 10$$
$$2a = 22$$
$$a = 11$$

Since only option B has a solution with 11 no further calculations are required.

95. C

$$810\frac{8}{9} = x$$
$$810(8) = 9x$$
$$6480 = 9x$$
$$x = 720$$

96. D

$$(2x + 5)(3x^2 - 2x - 4) =$$
$$= 6x^3 - 4x^2 - 8x + 15x^2 - 10x - 20$$
$$= 6x^3 + 11x^2 - 18x - 20$$

97. D

$$2(x^2 - 4x - 12)$$
$$2(x - 6)(x + 2)$$

98. B

$$\frac{18}{100} \, 1200 = x$$
$$18(1200) = 100x$$
$$21600 = 100x$$
$$x = 216$$

99. A

$$\frac{y_2 - y_1}{x_2 - x_1} =$$
$$= \frac{2 - 18}{5 - (-3)}$$
$$= \frac{-16}{8}$$
$$= -2$$

100. C

A perpendicular line will have a slope that is −1/m to the original line. The given equation is in standard from: y=mx+b, therefore we are looking for a line that has a slope of:

$$\frac{-1}{m} =$$
$$= \frac{-1}{-5} = \frac{1}{5}$$

Only option C has a slope of this value.

101. B

$$R := \frac{S}{2}$$
$$S := 3T$$
$$R + S + T := 55$$

Substitute the top two equations into the bottom one and solve for T:

$$\frac{S}{T} + 3T + T = 55$$

$$\frac{3T}{2} + 3T + T = 55$$

$$\frac{3T}{2} + 4T = 55$$
$$3T + 8T = 110$$
$$11T = 110$$
$$T = 10$$

102. B

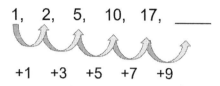

103. C

$$(2x^4)(3x^6) =$$
$$= (2 \times 3)x^{(4+6)}$$
$$= 6x^{10}$$

104. A

$$\frac{10}{100}\,62(4) = x$$

$$10(62)(4) = 100x$$
$$2480 = 100x$$
$$x = 24.80$$

105. A

$$6(x^2 - 1) =$$
$$= 6(x^2 - 1)$$
$$= 6(x + 1)(x - 1)$$

106. B

$$3(2x + 6) + 2x = 10$$
$$6x + 18 + 2x = 10$$
$$8x + 18 = 10$$
$$8x = -8$$
$$x = -1$$

107. D

$$\frac{4}{5}\,60 =$$
$$= \frac{240}{5}$$
$$= 48$$

108. D

$$12(84 - 5) - (3 \times 54) =$$
$$= 12(79) - 162$$
$$= 948 - 162$$
$$= 786$$

109. B

Multiply the top equation by 2 and add the equations together

$$2(2x - 3y = 0)$$
$$+ \quad -4x + 2y = -8$$

$$4x - 6y = 0)$$
$$+ \quad -4x + 2y = -8$$
$$\overline{\quad -4y = -8}$$

$$y = 2$$

110. D

$$\frac{8}{20} =$$
$$= \frac{8 \times 5}{20 \times 5}$$
$$= \frac{40}{100}$$

111. C

$$\begin{array}{r} 27 \\ \times \quad 2.5 \\ \hline 135 \\ + \quad 540 \\ \hline 67.5 \end{array}$$

112. D

$$y = 3(1)(2) + 2(2^3)$$
$$= 6 + 2(8)$$
$$= 6 + 16$$
$$= 22$$

113. D

$$3x^3y^5 + 3x^5y^3 - (4x^5y^3 - 3x^3y^5) =$$
$$= 3x^3y^5 + 3x^5y^3 - 4x^5y^3 + 3x^3y^5$$
$$= 6x^3y^5 - x^5y^3$$

114. D

$$\frac{45}{100} = \frac{9}{20}$$

115. B

Parallel lines will have the same slope, which leaves choices B & C. Using the given point we can find the equation using:

$$y - y_1 = m(x - x_1)$$
$$y - 1 = 4(x - 4)$$
$$y - 1 = 4x - 16$$
$$y = 4x - 15$$

116. B
117. C

$$\begin{array}{r} 14.72 \\ 23 \overline{\smash{)}338.56} \\ \underline{23} \\ 108 \\ \underline{92} \\ 165 \\ \underline{161} \\ 46 \\ \underline{46} \\ 0 \end{array}$$

118. D

$$\frac{12}{100}\ 15 = x$$
$$12(15) = 100x$$
$$180 = 100x$$
$$x = 1.80$$

119. C

$$\frac{80x}{100} = 44$$
$$80x = 4400$$
$$x = 55$$

120. B

$$V = LWH = 9(25)(15) = 3375$$

121. A

$$\frac{x_2 + x_1}{2}, \frac{y_2 + y_1}{2}$$
$$\frac{-20 + 4}{2}, \frac{4 + 8}{2}$$
$$\frac{-16}{2}, \frac{12}{2}$$
$$-8, 6$$

122. B

$$\frac{8}{72} = \frac{x}{72}$$
$$8(72) = 24x$$
$$576 = 24x$$
$$x = 24$$

123. D

Calculate how much the car depreciates each year.
$$\frac{12}{100} 7250 = x$$
$$12(7250) = 100x$$
$$87000 = 100x$$
$$x = 870$$
Subtract the depreciation amount from the cost.
$$7250 - 870 = 6380$$

124. A

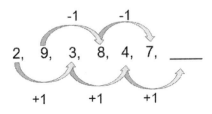

125. B

$$3(x + 5)(x - 2) =$$
$$= 3(5x - 10 + x^2 - 2x)$$
$$= 3(x^2 + 3x - 10)$$
$$= 3x^2 + 9x - 30$$

126. D

$$5 \div \frac{30}{36} =$$
$$= 5 \div \frac{5}{6}$$
$$= 5 \times \frac{6}{5}$$
$$= \frac{30}{5}$$
$$= 6$$

127. D

$$L = \frac{2F}{a}$$
$$F = b$$

$$L = \frac{2F}{a} = \frac{2b}{a}$$

128. B

$$\frac{30}{100} 40 = x$$
$$30(40) = 100x$$
$$1200 = 100x$$
$$x = 12$$

129. C

$$5^{11} = 5^2 \times 5^x$$
$$5^{11} = 5^{2+x}$$
$$11 = 2 + x$$
$$x = 9$$

130. B
131. A

$$3(2x + 7y = 4)$$
$$2(3x + 5y = -5)$$

$$6x + 21y = 12$$
$$-\ 6x + 10y = -10$$
$$11y = 22$$
$$y = 2$$

Plug the value of y into one of the original equations and solve for x

$$3x + 5(2) = -5$$
$$3x + 10 = -5$$
$$3x = -15$$
$$x = -5$$

132. D

$$(7y^2 + 3xy - 9) - (2y^2 + 3xy - 5) =$$
$$= 7y^2 + 3xy - 9 - 2y^2 - 3xy + 5$$
$$= 5y^2 - 4$$

133. B
134. D

$$\frac{x}{-4} + 3 = -7$$
$$\frac{x}{-4} = -10$$
$$x = 40$$

135. B

First, calculate the slope
$$\frac{y_2 - y_1}{x_2 - x_1} =$$
$$= \frac{3 - (-1)}{2 - 0}$$
$$= \frac{4}{2}$$
$$= 2$$

We can use the point slop formula to determine the equation of the line.
$$y - y_1 = m(x - x_1)$$
$$y - (-1) = 2(x - 0)$$
$$y + 1 = 2x$$
$$y = 2x - 1$$

136. A

$$\frac{24}{100} = \frac{6}{25}$$

137. C

$$\frac{6400}{400} = 16$$

138. D

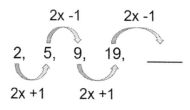

139. B

$$\frac{8}{26} = \frac{37}{x}$$
$$8x = 26(37)$$
$$8x = 962$$
$$x = 120.25$$

140. D

$$\begin{array}{r} 250 \\ \times \quad 0.97 \\ \hline 3640 \\ 46800 \\ \hline 504.40 \end{array}$$

141. C

$$\frac{22}{100} \, 150 = x$$

$$22(150) = 100x$$
$$3300 = 100x$$
$$x = 33$$

142. B

Calculate the total length of the chain in inches
$$3.5(12) = 42$$
Multiply the length by the cost per an inch.

$$42(0.14) = 5.88$$

143. A

$$\frac{\text{yellow} + \text{green}}{\text{total}} = \frac{26 + 19}{105} = \frac{45}{105} = \frac{3}{7}$$

144. B

$$\sqrt{6^2 + 8^2} =$$
$$= \sqrt{36 + 64}$$
$$= \sqrt{100}$$
$$= 10$$

145. C

$$\frac{42.5}{100} \, 200 = x$$
$$42.5(200) = 100x$$
$$8500 = 100x$$
$$x = 85$$

146. D

$$(3x^4 + 3x^2 - x + 5) - 3(x^4 + x^3 - 2x^2 - 6) =$$
$$= 3x^4 + 3x^2 - x + 5 - 3x^4 - 3x^3 + 6x^2 + 18$$
$$= -3x^3 + 9x^2 - x + 23$$

147. C

$$\begin{array}{r} 60 \\ \hline 6\,)\,540 \\ 54 \\ \hline 0 \end{array}$$

148. B

$$2(4a + b = 5)$$
$$- \quad 8a + 2b = -6$$

$$8a + 2b = 10$$
$$- \quad 8a + 2b = -6$$

There are no solutions as no value of a and b will satisfy both equations simultaneously. This is because the left side of the equation is the same, but the right side is different.

149. A

$$\frac{1}{3x} + \frac{5}{12} = \frac{2}{x}$$

$$\frac{5}{12} = \frac{2}{x} - \frac{1}{3x}$$

$$\frac{5x}{12} = 2 - \frac{1}{3}$$

$$5x = 24 - 4$$

$$5x = 20$$

$$x = 4$$

150. C

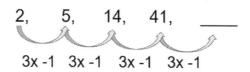

151. D
152. B
153. C
154. A
155. D
156. A
157. C
158. D
159. D
160. A
161. B
162. D
163. D
164. A
165. B
166. C
167. D
168. B
169. C
170. A
171. C
172. D
173. C
174. A
175. C
176. A

177. D
178. B
179. D
180. A
181. C
182. C
183. C
184. D
185. A
186. C
187. B
188. D
189. D
190. C
191. A
192. D
193. B
194. A
195. B
196. C
197. C
198. D
199. B
200. A
201. C
202. B
203. C
204. A
205. D
206. A
207. B
208. D
209. A
210. C
211. C
212. A
213. C
214. A
215. B
216. B
217. C
218. C

219. A
220. A
221. D
222. B
223. D
224. C
225. D
226. B
227. A
228. D
229. C
230. B
231. D
232. A
233. B
234. D
235. A
236. D
237. D
238. C
239. B
240. D
241. A
242. C
243. D
244. A
245. C
246. C
247. B
248. D
249. B
250. D
251. B
252. B
253. D
254. A
255. B
256. D
257. C
258. D
259. B
260. A

261. C
262. B
263. C
264. B
265. A
266. C
267. C
268. A
269. D
270. C
271. B
272. C
273. D
274. A
275. C
276. B
277. A
278. C
279. B
280. D
281. B
282. A
283. B
284. D
285. A
286. C
287. C
288. A
289. D
290. B
291. C
292. A
293. C
294. D
295. A
296. C
297. D
298. A
299. B
300. D

Made in the USA
Monee, IL
16 September 2024

65935122R00055